THE SACRED CAT OF BURMA CENTENNIAL

(1923-2023)

Alaln Lescart

AMRYL

Copyright © 2023 Alain Lescart

All rights reserved

The characters and events portrayed in this book are fictitious. Any similarity to real persons, living or dead, is coincidental and not intended by the author.

No part of this book may be reproduced, or stored in a retrieval system, or transmitted in any form or by any means, electronic, mechanical, photocopying, recording, or otherwise, without express written permission of the publisher.

ISBN-13: 9798872192169

Cover design by: Art Painter
Library of Congress Control Number: 2018675309
Printed in the United States of America

CONTENTS

Title Page	
Copyright	
Acknowledgment	1
A Mysterious Tale	4
An Indochinese Story	7
The Golden Legend	10
The Most Expensive Cat	14
A Crooked Story	16
An Enigmatic Inheritance	18
The Investigation	21
Origin	25
The arrival of the first Siamese in Europe	27
The First Birmans	29
Birman: 1930 Standard	37
Birman: FiFe Standard 2016	38
The Birman Ancestors	39
Creation of Colors Throughout the Ages.	46
Birman Genetic: Colors	67
The Centennial Pictures	73
Bibliography	105
Books In This Series	107
Books By This Author	109
About The Author	111

ACKNOWLEDGMENT

I would like to express my special thanks to Mrs. Janine Soumaille and the Sacred Birman Cat Club (FiFe) of France, who organized the Special Birmans Exhibition in March 2023 with great skill and heartfelt generosity, especially on the occasion of the centennial celebration of this extraordinary cat breed.

I also extend my gratitude to Mrs. Michèle Lefrançois for her presentation on the nuances of the Birman and her systematic work toward the improvement of the breed.

A MYSTERIOUS TALE

It's a somewhat adventurous, epic, and mysterious tale that unveils the enigmatic appearance of the Sacred Birman Cat in France. This revelation initially occurred within the exclusive circle of the early promoters of feline exhibitions in France during the 1920s. The orchestrators of these exhibitions were the young veterinarian Philippe Jumaud, who, in 1925, published his doctoral thesis and one of the first books on Cat Breeds (Jumaud), and Mrs. Marcelle Adam, well-known at that time for her literary contributions and serial publications in popular daily newspapers.

Indeed, the French public officially discovered the existence of the Sacred Birman Cat on December 26, 1925, by consulting the bottom of page 5 of the newspaper *Le Matin*. In a serialized novel titled "L'Amour qui tremble" (Love that Shakes), Mrs. Marcelle Adam described:

> *"But here, at the level of the pillow, Etienne sees a small brown mask with blue eyes. Two otter paws with white fingers stretch out of the bed, a purring unravels like a spinning wheel. [...] He pulls towards him a wonderful creature. Long ivory silks, streaked with gold on the back, a crest disheveled like a brown ostrich feather, a dark face illuminated by two sapphires of an unheard-of blue. In short, except for the immaculate gloves on the dark paws, the nuances of Siamese cats. But this supple body, this fur, loosely undulated, this snub nose of a griffin, this bulging forehead, these intensely azure eyes mark the Sacred Birman Cat. [...] Hiram-Roi is undoubtedly, in*

France, the only specimen of this precious breed. The writer received the homage of a British officer. [And further] ... Hiram-Roi fixes his sapphire gaze on her, meditative and nostalgic, where a secret seems to sleep" (Adam).

---

41. — Feuilleton du MATIN du 26 déc.

L'amour qui tremble

ROMAN
MARCELLE ADAM

PREMIÈRE PARTIE

L'AMOUR DANS LES MYRTES

V.

Etienne, d'abord, voit un titre : *Abel et Caïn*. Il comprend. Une fois déjà il aperçut ce manuscrit où, tout palpitant, le cœur de Pascal est cloué. Il lit. Une sueur d'angoisse mouille son front. C'est le halètement d'une âme, affolée comme un oiseau nocturne devant la lumière, c'est la clameur du conquérant, les plaintes du vaincu. Heures d'amour, heures d'extase, heures ferventes, heures cruelles. Et, sur tout cela, le mensonge, éprouvé du remords, les paroles trompeuses, les gestes hypocrites, le désir masqué d'innocence, la haine au sourire faux. La lutte enfin, la lutte éternelle du mal contre le bien, le cœur déchirant son frère et baisant ses blessures, le combat entre les forces multiples qui sont en nous, la chute après l'envol, la beauté criminelle de la femme armant Caïn. Le vin généreux des rêves, les voluptés cruelles et douces, la souffrance infinie, les craintes, les peurs, le reniement de l'amour, les sacrifices réprouvés, tous les tourments d'Abel, toutes les tristesses d'Abel. Oh ! cette jalousie, plus aiguë d'être fraternelle, cette rancune née dans la confiance, cette colère où l'estime se dresse aux côtés de l'admiration ! Et le meurtre dont ne se console plus le meurtrier, le meurtre où l'amour, un instant, se régénère, pour fuir ensuite de dégoût.

Jamais Pascal n'atteignit une telle puissance. Sa forme demeure parfaite et, selon sa manière très personnelle, le lyrisme s'y lie étroitement à la vérité. Ces pages sont l'analyse minutieuse d'un martyr qui se regarde agoniser, notant chaque cri, chaque soubresaut, chaque apaisement, chaque lièvre.

Quand il a fini de lire, le médecin reste longtemps dans une immobilité de statue. L'horreur et l'émerveillement montent, en désordre, de son cœur à son cerveau. Il est triste infiniment. Il voudrait savoir que Pascal lui pardonne les tortures dont il est la cause involontaire ; il voudrait recueillir la pensée qui vient de se livrer et, courbé sur elle, l'apaiser, comme il fait du corps qu'une amie de ses tumultes. Puis l'image de Sylvine glisse doucement devant lui. La belle fille au sourire arqué l... Hélas ! pourquoi donc a-t-elle ressuscité pour Lélia de la *Forêt de myrtes* ? Que n'est-elle restée, incertaine et fluide, au lointain pays des souvenirs ?

Etienne, à demi-voix, formule une réponse.

— Il fallait peut-être cela pour que Pascal écrivît un tel livre.

— De quel livre parles-tu ? demande le malade.

Etienne, alors, s'arrache à son émoi. Il vient vers son ami.

— Mon pauvre vieux, dit-il, nous sommes bien malheureux.

— Peux-tu ne pas me détester ?

— Pourrais-je ne pas t'aimer ? Ecoute-moi bien. Je vais, dès demain, emmener Sylvine, puisque ma mission est accomplie...

— Tais-toi. Je vais emmener Sylvine et tu continueras de la guérir. Voici deux mois, la faiblesse te suggérait des idées folles. La réalité n'est pas celle que tu crains. Tu achèveras de le soigner. La vie est une grâce à laquelle on se cramponne d'autant plus qu'elle fait souffrir. Mais oui, nous connaissons cela, nous autres phtisiques ; le bonheur affadit. On se lasse de lui, paraît-il, à la longue. La couleur enfuit les âmes. Dans un an, dans deux ans, tu béniras celle qui t'a dicté ces pages extraordinaires.

Pascal éclate d'un rire triste.

— Ton indulgence est infinie parce qu'elle s'adresse à un moribond. Qu'ai-je encore à vivre ? Un an, disent demain, peut-être, serai-je à la merci d'une nouvelle hémoptysie.

Etienne, désespéré, lui crie :

— Je te jure...

Mais l'écrivain lui coupe la parole :

— Est-ce pitoyable de me prolonger ?

— Je te jure que ton poumon cicatrisé, tu seras robuste et sans défaillance. Ton œuvre n'est pas terminée. Ce livre-ci en marque l'apogée.

Pascal s'irrite, la tête enfouie dans l'oreiller.

— Ce livre-ci, je vais le brûler tout à l'heure. Penses-tu que je vais me prostituer de la sorte, livrer mon cœur en pâture au public ? Distraire la foule au spectacle de nos tourments ? Divulguer notre intimité, nos discussions, nos remords ? Exposer Sylvine sans voiles à la curiosité des badauds ? Si tu le souhaites, mon cher, c'est que les sentiments pour elle ne valent pas les miens.

Etienne sourit :

— Donne-les-moi, demande Etienne.

— Non, non, remets-les dans leur tiroir. Je veux, tu entends, je veux...

Une mauvaise lueur s'allume au fond de ses yeux ; il tord nerveusement ses mains amaigries et ses pommettes rougissent. Le docteur obéit, à regret.

— Alors, reprend Pascal, vous partirez demain... tous les deux ?

— Sans doute, nous partirons, puisque c'est nécessaire. Je songe à conduire Sylvine en Bretagne, où nous nous marierons. Ensuite, n'est-ce pas, mon vieux, tu seras son ami, notre ami ?

L'écrivain cache son front sous ses couvertures et ne répond pas. Etienne se penche encore :

— Voyons, Pascal... Voyons, mon vieux.

Mais voici que, à la hauteur de l'oreiller, il aperçoit un petit masque brun aux yeux bleus. Deux pattes loutres aux doigts blancs s'étirent hors du lit, un ronronnement se dévide à la manière d'un rouet.

— Quoi ! s'écrie le docteur, tu as encore couché Hiram avec toi cette nuit. Je t'ai pourtant défendu cela ?

Il tire à lui une bête merveilleuse. Longues soies ivoirines, se striant d'or sur l'échine, panache éploré comme une plume d'autruche de couleur marron, visage sombre éclairé par deux saphirs d'un bleu inouï. Bref, sauf les gants immaculés sur les pattes foncées, les nuances des chats de Siam. Mais ce corps souple, cette fourrure largement ondée, ce nez camus de griffon belge, ce front bombé, ces yeux d'azur intense marquent le chat sacré de Birmanie, dont Pascal est très fier. Hiram-Roi, sans doute, est, en France, le seul spécimen de cette race précieuse. L'écrivain en a reçu l'hommage d'un officier britannique. Les gens de lettres et les artistes se plaisent dans la société des jolis dieux pénates, aux yeux de clair de lune. « O Hamilcar, gardien silencieux de la Cité des livres ! »... murmure Sylvestre Bonnard à son ami griffu.

Etienne pose sur le tapis Hiram-Roi et l'eau des yeux d'azur devient noire. Pascal observe le médecin.

— Tes craintes sont-elles pour lui ou pour moi ?

Le docteur se tait. Il regarde un instant le malade et lui dit :

— Crois en moi comme je crois en toi. Ta route sera longue et belle. Dis donc, tu vas te lever et descendre au jardin. Il fait un temps délicieux. Je me rends à Paris et ne reviendrai que demain, à cause de mes malades et de mon hôpital. Sois calme et sois prudent. Crois en moi.

**

Chacun est trop gai, durant ce déjeuner. Les rires sonnent faux comme les notes d'un instrument désaccordé ; les paroles ne répondent pas aux pensées qui s'épient sans s'exprimer ; les sourires mentent ; les regards se taisent. Sylvine a dit, d'un air distrait :

— Vous savez, il me faut partir demain. Dès septembre, je répèterai Mélisande, à l'Opéra-Comique. J'ai beaucoup à travailler.

Mme Gerboise, qui n'ignore rien des secrets de son fils, baisse la tête et répond :

— Que c'est regrettable ! Vous vous en allez trop tôt.

Mme Larsay, avec une politesse glacée, murmure :

— Nous devons nous ranger aux raisons de Mlle Grazielli.

Pascal, d'une voix sans timbre, ajoute :

— Sylvine est sage... à moins qu'elle ne soit insensée. Qu'est-ce que la sagesse ?

Dès lors, tous quatre, ils se sont efforcés vers des propos indifférents. Ils s'y maintiennent ensuite, ainsi que des promeneurs suivent les grandes routes, par peur des chemins de traverse, semés d'embûches. Le repas fini, Sylvine se met au piano. Elle chante toute la nostalgie de l'âme russe exprimée par Moussorgsky. Pascal, qui l'écoute, le tempo de voir cette brève rencontre, l'interrompt violemment :

— Assez... assez... cette musique est trop triste. Elle m'étouffe aujourd'hui.

— Pourquoi, demanda Sylvine, n'êtes-vous point au jardin par ce soleil ?

Il se récrie :

— Voulez-vous me voler les dernières heures que vous nous accordez ?

— Ne soyez pas méchante, dit railleusement Mme Larsay.

Elle contraint au silence le chagrin qui la tord. Comme elle se sent seule parmi ces gens ! Mais chacun d'eux n'est-il pas seul ? Les âmes se cherchent sans se trouver jamais. Parfois, une brève rencontre, le temps de voir les traits que voulait l'illusion. Ainsi cette Sylvine plaît à Pascal. Que sera-t-elle pour lui ? Une strophe du grand poème où les nobles chercheront son cœur. Une strophe, pas davantage, évidemment. Mais cette strophe l'égalera peut-être aux amantes immortelles dont elle se sent si loin, la pauvre Madeleine ! Le génie plane à de telles hauteurs qu'à l'apercevoir plus ceux qui restent dans la vallée. Pascal tente d'emporter Sylvine.

(A suivre.)

ALAIN LESCART

AN INDOCHINESE STORY

And indeed, there is a wealth of secrets, a tale to tell, and a spinning wheel to unravel beyond the purrs and leg rubs. Where does this enchanting and endearing aristocrat come from, clinging to our legs like a faithful shadow of our being?

Right from the very beginning of its history, a golden legend from Indochina clings to its existence. It takes flight from the depths of the Cambodian jungle to soar to the majestic heights of Burma.

This captivating narrative, skillfully recounted by Miss Marcelle Adam in her novel, newspaper articles, and interviews during the 1920s and 1930s, was handed down to her by the pioneer Birman breeder, Miss Juanita Léotardi. Since the years 1921-22, Miss Léotardi had been nurturing these enchanting creatures and passed on to the novelist-treasurer of the professional union of French Novelists and president of the Cat Club of Paris her very first Birman, Manou de Madalpour (born in 1925, and who, nine years later, would gracefully enter feline paradise). Manou caused a sensation at the inaugural feline exhibition in Paris in May 1926.

His black and white image, cradled in the majestic arms of the novelist, adorned the front page of newspapers covering this epic event, the very first grand feline exhibition in Paris.

(Photos *Petit Journal*)
Deux lauréats et leurs « mères »
En bas, un joli spécimen de chat de Birmanie

THE GOLDEN LEGEND

Here is a captivating legend that tells of the existence of a unique clandestine temple, perched atop the Burmese mountains. There, 100 monks lived in perfect harmony alongside their feline companions, united in the worship of a long-forgotten golden deity, whose eyes shimmer like sapphires. Madame Léotardi unequivocally asserts that a pair of these sacred cats was clandestinely taken from the watchful eyes of the monks and then exported to the Hexagon (France) by a British officer with a changing name, alternately Lesley and later Gordon.

The journey of these precious felines would have been as mysterious as their origin. Some say they were transported aboard the yacht of the famous American millionaire Harold Vanderbilt, while others recount even more astonishing adventures, plunging the narrative into a whirlwind of adventures where myth inexorably intertwines with reality. An evolving story that continues to transform, arousing the curiosity of all who delve into it.

> *"Long before the advent of the Buddha, long before the birth of Brahmanism, even before Vyâsa dictated the immortal words of his divine books, the Khmer people jealously guarded their temples, where the Kittahs, venerable priests so close to perfection that their spirit, before conquering eternal ecstasy, passed only into the body of a sacred cat for the duration of its animal existence. But from the origin of the worlds, the saints disapproved of those who did not sanctify themselves in*

their way. Thus did the Brahmins who attacked the Kittahs and devoutly massacred them. However, some of the venerable ones managed to escape through the inviolable mountains of northern Burma, and there they founded the underground temple of Lao-Tsun, which means the dwelling of the gods.

This temple is a marvel among the wonders of Indochina. Not far from a lake, it is lost in a chaos of immense peaks, and if, by an extraordinary favor, my English friend could enter, it is because he happened to protect the last Kittahs against the ruthless Brahmins. He could thus contemplate the hundred sacred cats of the cult and learn their history."

When, under the malevolent moon, the "phoums" or, if you prefer a clearer language, the accursed Siamese-Thais, those barbarians, arrived in the mountains of Lugh, in the mountains of the Sun, the most precious among the precious was at the temple of Lao-Tsun: the one whose god Song-Hio himself had woven the golden beard. The Venerable had always lived in contemplation of Tsun-Kyanksé, the goddess with sapphire eyes who presides over the transmutations of souls, whose number is counted. He never averted his gaze from her sculpted image. His name was Mun-Hâ. He had an oracle without which he made no decisions: his cat Sinh, whom the other Kittahs revered fervently."

Sinh, sitting near his dreaded master, also lived in contemplation of the goddess. The beautiful animal! His eyes were yellow as gold, yellow from the reflection of Mun-Hâ's metallic beard and the amber body of the goddess with sapphire eyes. One evening, at the moonrise, the Thais approached the sacred enclosure. Then, invoking the threatening Fate of his people, Mun-Hâ died laden with years and anxieties. He died in front of his goddess, with his divine cat by his side. And the Kittahs lamented such a cruel loss, under the threats of invasion. At that moment, the miracle of immediate transmutation occurred. Sinh leaped onto the holy throne, arching over his master's bowed head, facing the goddess. And the hairs of his white back became golden, and his eyes, his eyes yellow like the golds of Tsun-Kyanksé, yellow like the yellow of the beard woven by the god Song-Hio, his eyes turned blue. Immense and deep sapphires, resembling the idol's eyes. His four earth-brown paws, his four paws that touched the venerable skull, turned white, all the way to the purified fingertips touched by the powerful deceased. He turned his precious gaze towards the southern door, where a harsh, imperative order was read, to which, driven by an invincible force, the Kittahs obeyed. Thus, they closed the bronze doors of the holy temple to the ancestral enemy. Then, passing through their underground passages, they routed the desecrators. Sinh, refusing all food, never left the throne again. He stood facing the goddess, mysterious, hieratic, fixing his azure pupils on the sapphire eyes from which he took the flame and sweetness. Seven days after Mun-Hâ's death, standing on the purified white paws, without lowering his eyelids, he died, carrying Mun-Hâ's soul too perfect for earthly life towards Tsun-Kyanksé. But one last time, his gaze slowly turned towards the southern door, from where, later, the Annamite and Cambodian hordes would come in large numbers.

Seven days after Sinh's death, the Kittahs gathered before Tsun-Kyanksé to decide Mun-Hâ's succession. Then, oh wonder, they saw the hundred cats of the temple coming in a slow procession. Their paws were gloved in white, their snowy fur had golden reflections, and the topazes of their eyes had turned into sapphires. The Kittahs prostrated themselves in an attitude of devout awe. And they waited. Did they not know that the souls of their ancestors inhabited the harmonious forms of the sacred animals? These, solemn and supple, surrounded Ligoa, the youngest of the priests who thus knew the will of the sky.

THE MOST EXPENSIVE CAT

This uncertain origin, as captivating as it is enigmatic, did not take long to raise questions among the early breeders who sought to enhance their breeding. Journalists and explorers traversed Indochina in search of the slightest trace, without success. Despite growing doubts, Madame Adam clung with unwavering determination to the initial narrative, much like the early breeders who only partially subscribed to it. Thus, the legend of the Sacred Birman was born, transforming this enigmatic cat into the most precious animal of the pre-war era.

Indeed, one had to display colossal wealth and a pedigree befitting royalty to hope to lay hands on one of these enchanting cats, capable of captivating, corrupting, and even bewitching with a simple glance!

ON DIRAIT UN TOUAREG

Mme Léotardi dérobant son visage à l'objectif indiscret.

At the heart of this controversy, one person remained in the shadows, a mysterious puppeteer skillfully using others to promote the legend of the Sacred Birman and place her precious cats at exorbitant prices. This person was none other than the first breeder of Birmans, Madame Juanita Léotardi.

Abbé Chamonin (Marcel Reney), in his book "Nos Amis les Chats" in 1947, mentions this enigmatic figure:

> *"There was also, in their tale, a certain Madame Léotardi, a high-class adventurer, it seems, who had owned the Birmans after Madame Hadish... Madame Marcelle Adam, who surrounded the last days of Manou de Madalpour with her tender affection, told me in Paris that Madame Léotardi, before disappearing quite mysteriously, recounted the story of the Birmans as written by Jumaud and Baudoin."* (Reney and Abbé Chamonin, p. 178).

A story that becomes more complex as mysteries intertwine and the plot thickens.

DEUX INSTANTANÉS DE Mme LÉOTARDI, CACHANT SON VISAGE, ET M. LÉOTARDI, HIER, AU PALAIS

A CROOKED STORY

All efforts made to obtain information about this enigmatic woman had remained in vain until now. She appeared destined to linger in the impenetrable mists of time, carrying her secret with her to the grave.

However, the award of a research grant by my university, along with a sabbatical leave, finally paved the way for me to conduct in-depth investigations into this period and unveil the missing information about it.

I undertook a systematic approach, delving into the archives of daily newspapers from the 1920s at the National Library of France (BNF).

To my great astonishment, I discovered that the name of Madame Léotardi had made headlines in all French newspapers between 1922 and 1923, and again in 1931. This figure remarkably aligned with our mysterious Madame Léotardi, whose travels seemed to revolve around Nice and Paris.

Mme Léotardi à son arrivée au Palais.
(C'est en vain, comme on voit, qu'elle a tenté de se dérober à l'objectif de nos photographes.)

It was then that the outline of a story far more extraordinary than anticipated emerged before my eyes, revealing a mythomaniac and charlatan character endowed with disturbing charisma.
On December 22, 1922, France discovered the existence of a vast fraud that would become famous as "L'Affaire Léotardi." It captivated public opinion for three weeks, with daily twists and turns, providing material for a scandal worthy of Hollywood.

Mr. Bangue, a banker from the ninth arrondissement of Paris, filed a complaint against the Léotardi couple for obtaining an advance of 35,000 francs (equivalent to 23,450 euros today) from him, supposedly intended to cover the inheritance expenses of the late Miss Lilian Fair Heller, who died on July 21, 1921, aboard her yacht "Old Chap" during a cruise in the Mediterranean.

This deceased woman would have appointed Madame Léotardi as the universal legatee. However, as the case has been dragging on for more than 17 months without resolution and the body of the alleged deceased remains unfound, the banker begins to fear that this inheritance is nothing but pure fiction!

Other similar cases subsequently emerge, all linked to Madame Léotardi. The plot thickens, unveiling a narrative as tumultuous as it is captivating.

AN ENIGMATIC INHERITANCE

The story takes flight in 1910 when Madame Juanita Manchado, originally from Spain, claims to have met a certain Miss Fair-Heller in Nice, an American billionaire heiress of a renowned Californian senator, and an animal enthusiast.

Out of pure friendship and because Madame Léotardi shared a deep affection for four-legged creatures, this immensely wealthy lady would have bequeathed a fabulous inheritance to our heroine to look after her beloved animals.

In 1910, Mrs. Léotardi allegedly met Mrs. Lilian Fair-Heller, an American millionaire who adored animals, on the French Riviera, specifically in Nice. Out of pure friendship and because Mrs. Léotardi shared her sentiments towards animals, Mrs. Fair-Heller supposedly left her a fabulous inheritance, the amount of which varies in newspapers between 85 and 700 million dollars (between 1 and 9 billion francs of that time). The will, registered in Marseille, is dated July 6, 1921, just two weeks before the presumed death of its author. Here is the text:

> *I leave for Mrs. Jane Manchado, now Mrs. Albert Léotardi, my jewelry, and all my fortune. She must take care of my animals, all my animals. I also appoint my cousin Wilbur Heller Ryerson from Boston to carry out these wishes, and I leave him my yacht, the Old Chap, with its contents as a memento. These wishes must be the only ones executed, rendering all others null and void. Signed: Lillian Fair-Heller. Boston, U.S.A.*

I'll spare you the details of this multi-faceted and suspenseful story, worthy of another serial, which you can discover in full in my book. A police investigation will unveil over 600 forged documents in Madame Léotardi's possession, bearing the signatures of well-known personalities, including Harold Vanderbilt, who was purportedly the brief fiancé of this young lady for several months. A narrative as thrilling as it is unbelievable, where deceptions and intrigues continually multiply.

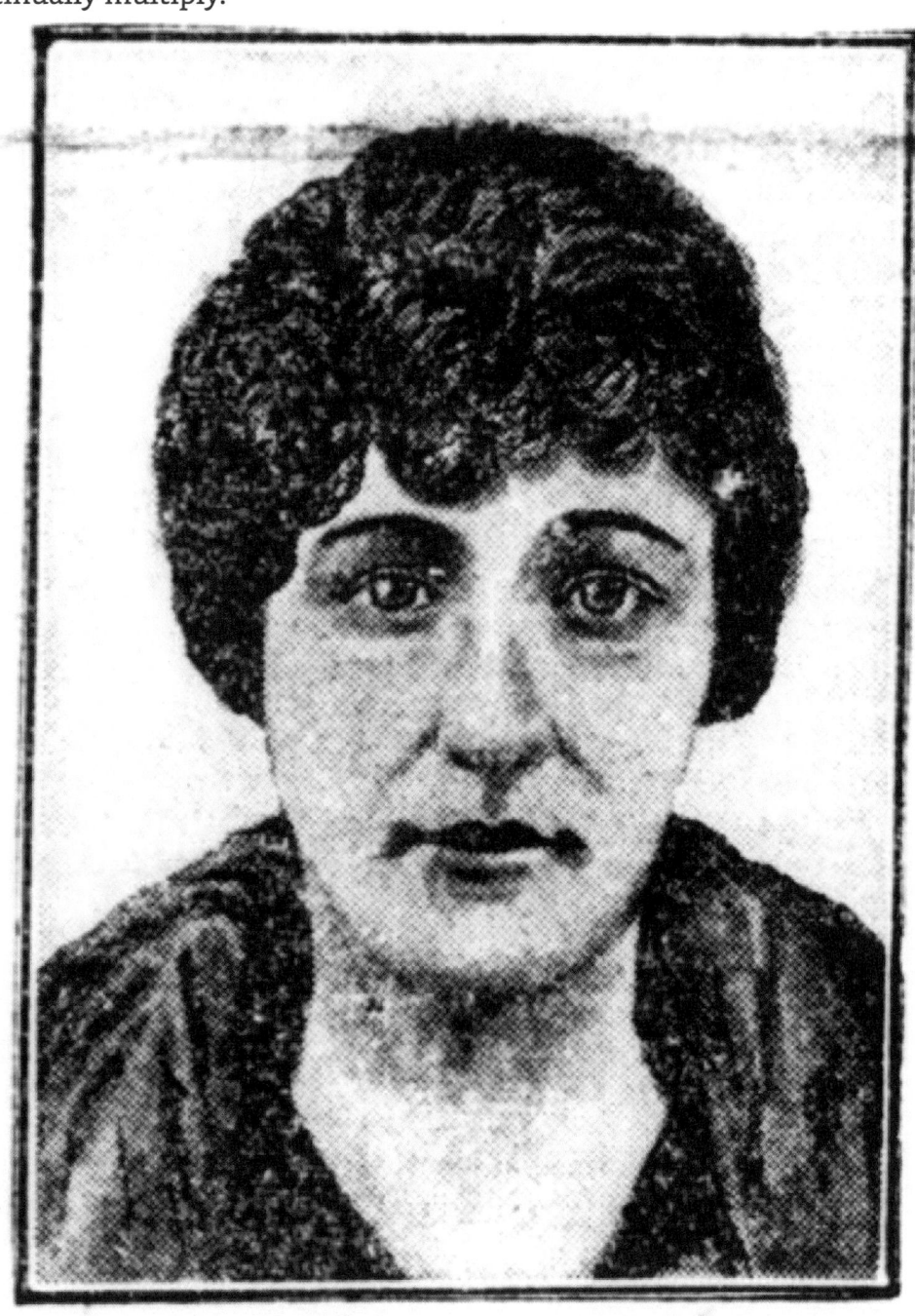

Mme LEOTARDI

prétendue héritière de miss Lillian Fair Heller, la milliardaire américaine

> **Mme Léotardi, héritière des fabuleux millions d'Amérique devant le tribunal correctionnel**

THE INVESTIGATION

Te investigation, which will span over a year with the intervention of the American consulate and will echo even in New York newspapers, will ultimately conclude with a monumental fraud. The American lady in question never existed, and the countless outlandish stories woven by Madame Juanita Léotardi prove to be pure fiction, despite her surprisingly persistent insistence that all forged documents are authentic.

It is Judge Barnaud who ultimately charges the Léotardi couple with fraud and complicity in fraud. Madame Léotardi's legal history, already sentenced to six months in prison in Nice in 1917 for another fraud case, comes back to haunt her.

Finally, on November 6, 1923, Madame Léotardi is arrested, but she is released for health reasons. However, on November 26, 1924, she is finally sentenced to one year in prison and a fine of 500 francs. She appeals and obtains a suspended sentence for a few years, but a final conviction occurs on January 17, 1927, doubling her initial sentence.

All these cases highlight the extraordinary audacity and composure of Madame Léotardi, who does not hesitate to produce fake documents, create imaginary characters, and even use the names of famous personalities she has never met, of course. Her charisma and acting talents, combined with a pathological tendency for mythomania (and the use of opium, according to a psychiatrist who examined her), allow her to maintain the mystery for years, whether it concerns the appearance of the Birman cat, whose story intertwines with that of the entirely invented fabulous inheritance.

Indeed, Madame Juanita Léotardi cleverly reuses some elements of these inheritance cases in her feline narrative. This is notably the case with the unfortunate Harold Vanderbilt, a signatory of forged checks to Madame Léotardi's address, but also the man who would have helped a temple servant acquire a pair of sacred cats.

The creation of imaginary characters is a constant between the two stories, as well as a small English town in Suffolk, Mildenhall. However, the climax of the parallel between the two fictions woven by Madame Léotardi lies in her recurring interest in animals. A story as fascinating as it is extraordinary, where reality and fiction blend strikingly.

Even more interestingly, on Saturday, December 23, 1922, in an interview with the newspaper La Liberté, Mrs. Léotardi used the "first Birman cat" to demonstrate her intimacy with the imaginary Miss Lilian Fair-Heller:

> *During a cruise with Miss Heller aboard her yacht Old Chap, we became quite intimate with her."*
>
> *– "Is it true that she [Miss Fair-Feler} had many animals around her?"*
>
> *– "My God! She had small dogs and cats, including the Birman cat here...*
>
> *And Mrs. Léotardi shows us a superb cat similar to Siamese cats, except that it is marked very curiously in white on all four paws." (Bard)*

In the eccentric imagination of Madame Juanita Léotardi, a new legend took shape, based on the idea that Miss Lilian Fair-Heller owned a collection of exotic animals scattered around the globe. According to this elaborate story, she would have acquired a cat stolen from a fictional Burmese temple through the mediation of her alleged lover at the time, Harold Vanderbilt. This cat would then have been offered to her imaginary fiancée.

However, after the trial and the revelation of the non-existence of Miss Fair-Heller, only Vanderbilt remained as a link in this chain, and the missing Miss Fair-Heller was replaced by a new equally fictional character: Miss Thadde Haddish, later accompanied by the equally elusive Major Russel Gordon.

Condemned again in 1931, this time for a necklace case, Madame Léotardi did not appear in court. She was again sentenced in absentia before completely disappearing from circulation. A story as fascinating as it is enigmatic, where the boundary between reality and fiction blurs in a spectacular way.

Mme Leotardi, héritière des fabuleux millions d'Amérique devant le tribunal correctionnel

Mme Leotardi, née Juanita Manchado, qui comparaissait hier devant la onzième chambre correctionnelle, sous la prévention d'escroquerie, se prétendait l'héritière d'une richissime américaine, miss Lilian Fair Heller, qui lui avait légué toute sa fortune, des millions de dollars et des millions de yen. Elle fit avec cette fable quelques dupes, trois exactement, qui, en tout et pour tout, lui apportèrent, par petits paquets, une centaine de mille francs.

Mme LEOTARDI

Née en 1886, à Barcelone, Mme Leotardi est une brune aux traits fins, tout de noir vêtue. Elle porte le deuil de son mari qui est mort au cours de l'instruction. C'est pourquoi elle est seule au banc des prévenus libres. Elle affirme, aujourd'hui encore, de sa voix douce, qui par moment veut être agressive, l'existence de miss Lilian Fair Heller. Elle fut son amie, à Nice, en 1918.

ORIGIN

If the Birman is not from Burma, where does it come from?

One thing is certain. The Birman has emerged from European Siamese lineages. Baudoin-Crevoisier openly declares in 1931:

'I know a superb Birman in terms of type, fur, eyes, tail, legs, and additionally, a perfect sire, which is the product of two Siamese. And it's not accidental; such cases often occur in the litters of these Siamese. [...] The Birman I mentioned earlier mated with a Siamese cat, the daughter of a Birman; the resulting offspring were almost all very beautiful Birmans, most of them with all four paws gauntleted, and some with only two paws. Among them, a male was perfect. The subsequent litters were also beautiful. In the Poupée line, which is essentially purebred, nothing better has been produced. There are very lightly gauntleted Birmans and even some with no gauntlets at all in this lineage.

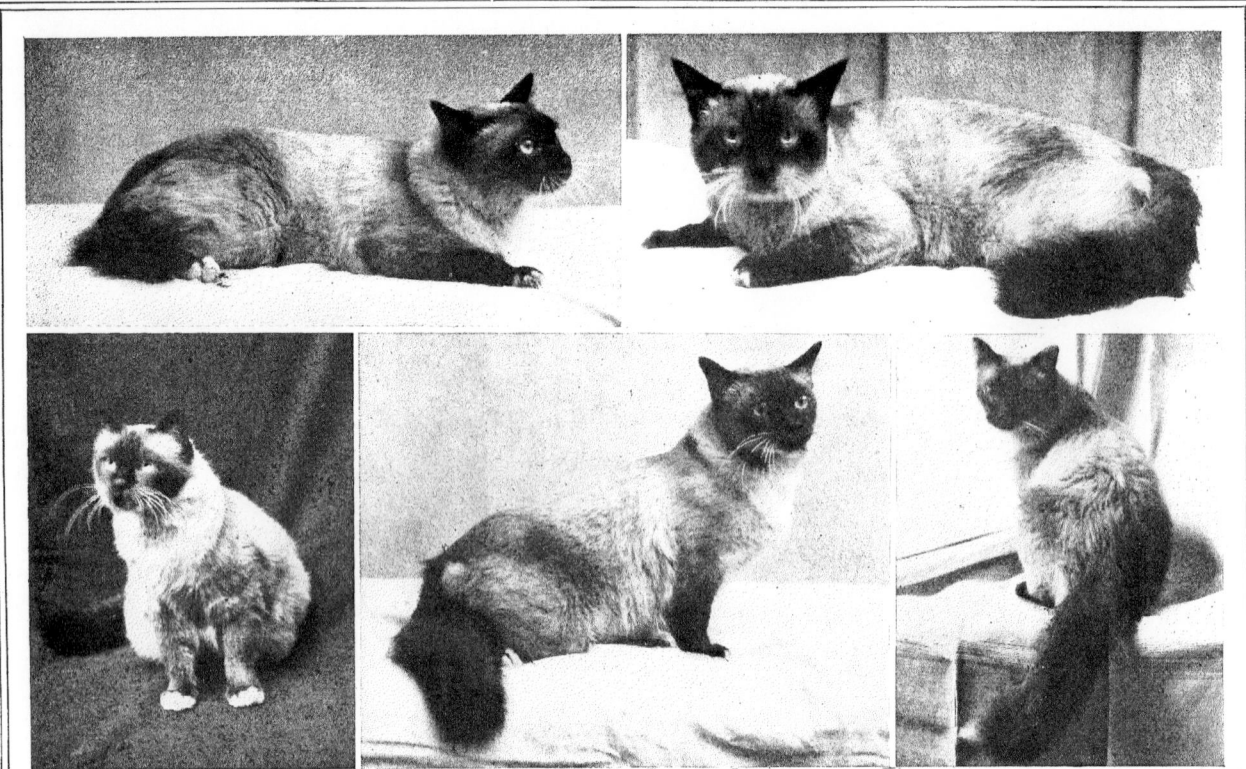

CHATS DE BIRMANIE. 1, 4 et 5. Manon de Madalpour, 1ᵉʳ prix Paris 1926; à Mme Marcelle Adam. 2 et 3. Poupée de Madalpour, jolie Chatte, 1ᵉʳ prix Paris 1926; à Mme Léotardi. Les sujets de cette race, au corps allongé, à la tête longue, aux yeux bleu de roi, à la robe garnie de poils longs et soyeux, se distinguent nettement des Chats asiatiques, avec lesquels ils ne sympathisent pas. Moins fougueux que les Siamois, ils sont très sociables, intelligents, gais, mais peu joueurs.

THE ARRIVAL OF THE FIRST SIAMESE IN EUROPE

To understand the emergence of these fascinating Birman cats in France, it is essential to delve into the history of Siamese cat breeding in Europe.

The first specimens of this breed appeared in France and England towards the end of the 19th century. Where did they come from? Primarily from Bangkok, Thailand.

During the summer of 1893, the *Jardin des Plantes* in Paris welcomed its first Siamese cats. They were the result of the dispatch of eight specimens by Auguste Pavie, an explorer and minister plenipotentiary of France to Laos, between 1893 and 1895. In total, twenty Siamese cats had taken up residence in the Jardin between 1893 and 1899, while Professor Alphonse Milne-Edwards, director of the National Museum of Natural History, started breeding Siamese cats in a former orangutan cage abandoned in 1896.

However, a dive into the archives of the *Jardin des Plantes* reveals that most of these imported Siamese cats met a sad fate, dying very quickly. The culprits? The lack of heating in the *Jardin des Plantes* during winter and the great fragility of these cats, poorly adapted to the climatic rigors of northern Europe. Fourteen of the twenty Siamese cats imported to the Jardin sadly perished during their first year, primarily victims of colds and chill.

The same scenario unfolded on the other side of the Channel in England, where Miss Frances Simpson declared in 1903 in her famous work "The Book of the Cat" that Siamese cats seemed more delicate than the most delicate long-haired cat breeds, with virtually no resistance to common diseases. She even lamented having seen adult specimens succumb to severe pneumonia in a flash, long before the first signs of the disease could be detected.

Twenty years later, in 1928, in her new book "Cats for Pleasure and Profits," she added that the most challenging breed to breed and maintain in the country was undoubtedly the Siamese. Some enthusiasts believed that these cats did not acclimate well to the European climate.

To solve this dilemma, European Siamese breeders had the ingenious idea of crossing these precious imported specimens with European white cats with blue eyes, creating more robust individuals. The Cat Club of the English Siamese attested that some breeders had successfully crossed a white male cat with blue eyes with a Siamese, giving birth to award-winning Siamese champions. Others did the same, suggesting that this strategy was beginning to bear fruit.

It is worth noting that the Siamese cats imported from Thailand came in two distinct varieties: the Royal Siamese Cat and the Temple Cat, under the responsibility of Jainist monks, with a more rounded morphology.

A true saga where men's passion for these fascinating felines gave rise to exciting new feline adventures in Europe.

By introducing a new cat with white genes into the imported Siamese lineages (which were not always pure, to begin with), new recessive genes were added to the genetic heritage. Siamese breeders occasionally observed the manifestation of these crossbred genes, characterized by longer fur—which would later give rise to the Balinese cat (a long-haired Siamese)—and the appearance of additional white gloves. This explains the origin of the Sacred Birman Cat, which reinforced these genes and established them in the breeding of a new breed.

THE FIRST BIRMANS

At the heart of the birth of this noble feline breed, two cats emerge like legends: first, the first breeding female, the matrix of the breed, **Poupée de Madalpour**; then the male who would perpetuate generations to come, **Hiram-Roi de Madalpour**, born at the end of the year 1924 and the father of Manou de Madalpour.

While history has preserved many photographs of *Poupée,* only one image of *Hiram-Roi* remains. He was born from the union of Poupée and a Siamese cat carrying the long-haired gene, nicknamed the "Laos Cat."

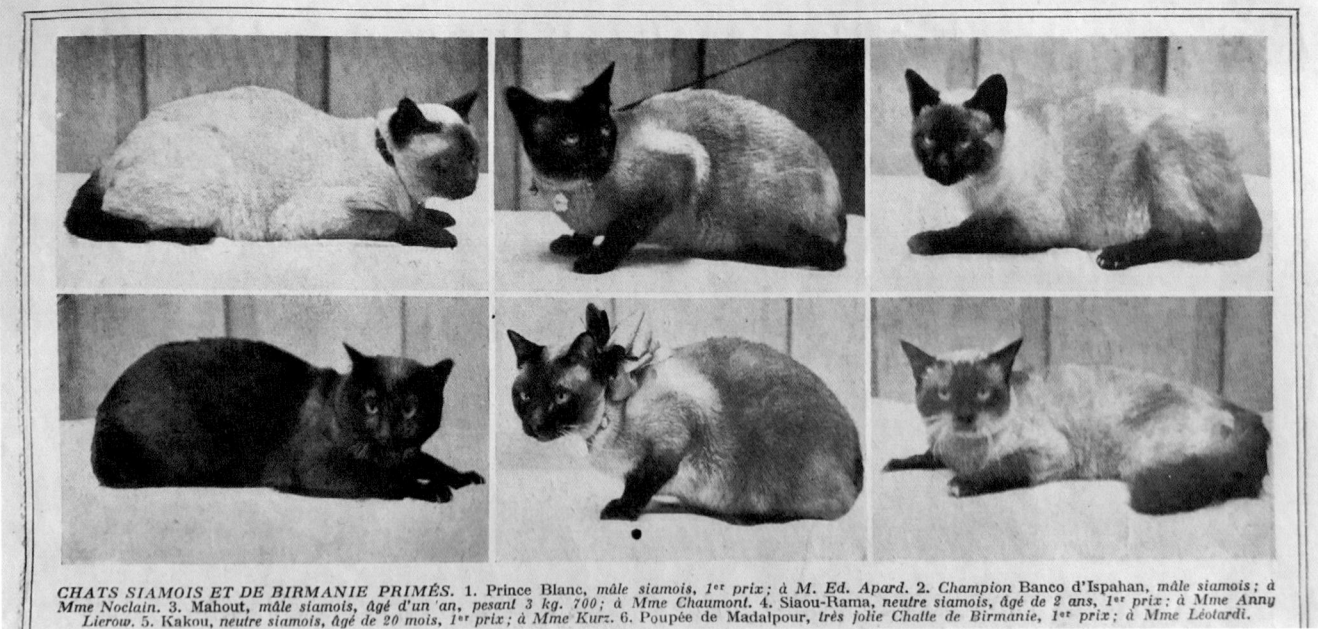

CHATS SIAMOIS ET DE BIRMANIE PRIMÉS. 1. Prince Blanc, mâle siamois, 1er prix; à M. Ed. Apard. 2. Champion Banco d'Ispahan, mâle siamois; à Mme Noclain. 3. Mahout, mâle siamois, âgé d'un an, pesant 3 kg. 700; à Mme Chaumont. 4. Siaou-Rama, neutre siamois, âgé de 2 ans, 1er prix; à Mme Anny Lierow. 5. Kakou, neutre siamois, âgé de 20 mois, 1er prix; à Mme Kurz. 6. Poupée de Madalpour, très jolie Chatte de Birmanie, 1er prix; à Mme Léotardi.

At first glance, *Poupée* shares many similarities with the seal-point Siamese of that time. A photo from 1926 shows her alongside victorious Siamese, revealing a strong kinship between the two breeds, with the notable exception of slightly longer fur, a slightly rounder head, a majestic tail, eyes of a captivating deep blue, and small white gloves at the tips of her paws.

To ensure the offspring, a true phalanx of these special felines was formed, always returning to the same lineages. What had made the success of this breeding turned into a real tragedy, as excessive inbreeding eventually led to many fragile and vulnerable individuals. Madame Léotardi herself admitted that she could only obtain one kitten out of ten.

A true epic, where passion for the preservation of this unique breed defied the most arduous trials and challenges.

Among the cat breeders who revolved around Mrs. Leotardi during her early exhibitions, a prominent figure emerges : *Mrs. Brassart*, originally from Pas-de-Calais. She was the largest Persian breeder in France with her *Maritza* cattery and was among the organizers of the Paris cat show in 1927.

Fascinated by the history of the Birman, she was the first to engage in the breeding of this breed, in collaboration with *Mrs. Max Gibert*, who exhibited **Nafaghi** and **Bijou** de Madalpour. Mrs. Brassart gave birth to one of the most beautiful Birmans of that time in 1928: **Lon Saïto de Madalpour**, whose photo is featured in Jumaud's "Les Races de Chats" published in 1930.

Chat de Birmanie à Mme Brassart

It is also worth mentioning *Mrs. de Marigny*, who joined the adventure in 1930 by producing the famous Djaïpour de Madalpour before withdrawing from breeding after two years of dedicated efforts.

From 1928, another personality, *Mrs. Madeleine Boyer,* acquired Fly de Kaabaa, a hybrid Birman produced by *Mrs. Gilles-Lenaerts*. She adopted the affix name **Kaabaa,** although her name does not appear in pre-war exhibition reports.

A constellation of passionate breeders gathered to preserve this precious feline breed, writing together the history of the Sacred Birman Cat. An adventure rich in challenges and successes, marked by dedication and love for these extraordinary felines.

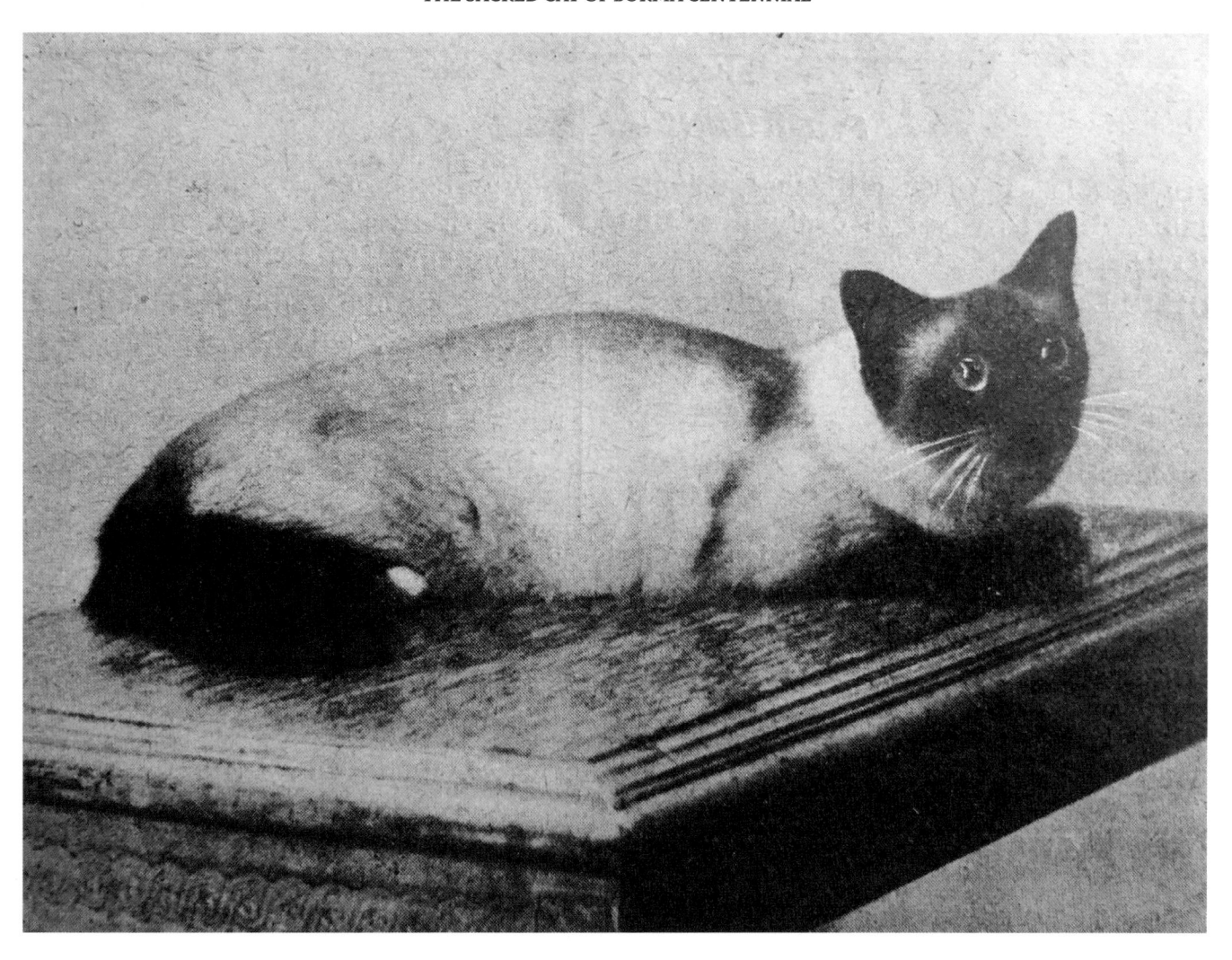

In 1931, a new prominent figure enters the feline breeding scene: *Mrs. Chaumont Doizy*, a renowned Siamese breeder. She represents one of the two lines that will survive the war and from which our precious Birmans today descend.

Her Siamese achievements were already featured alongside Poupée in the photo of the first exhibition in 1926. In addition to her Siamese, she also raised some Persians, placing her in an ideal position to venture into Birman breeding.

Later, she would take up the **Madalpour** affix, thus inscribing her name in the exciting history of this extraordinary feline breed. A new era begins for the Birman, under the leadership of a determined and passionate breeder who will greatly contribute to the evolution and perpetuity of this unique breed.

Finally, in 1931, a new Parisian breeder, *Mr. Marcel Baudoin-Crevoisier*, who had started his venture in 1929, boldly entered into Birman breeding. Unafraid to diversify the lineages by crossing with other Siamese and Persian strains, under his guidance, the most splendid representatives of the pre-war Birman are born, creating a new line that breathes new life into this extraordinary breed.

God of Arakan and **Queen of Rangoon**, names that resonate like legends, win all votes, and initiate a transformation that brings these Birmans closer to the modern specimens we know today.

It is a time of renewal and metamorphosis for this feline breed, where Marcel Baudoin-Crevoisier becomes the master of this rebirth, creating a lineage that will endure through generations.

Chat sacré de Birmanie
" DIEU D'ARAKAN ", Champion international à M. Baudoin (C. C. P.).
Un des plus magnifiques parmi les très rares spécimens de cette race mystérieuse actuellement en Europe.

A new and exciting chapter of the Birman's history unfolds, carried by the ingenuity and determination of this visionary breeder.

The Birman breed is then distributed into four distinct lines, each carrying the heritage of a fascinating history. The Madalpour, direct descendants of Poupée, write their chapter in the Birman narrative. With Crevoisier, the Arakan, Rangoon, and Mandalay lines emerge, each bringing its own flavor to this ever-evolving story.

In 1931, five cats turn heads and captivate admiring looks: Lon Saïto, God of Arakan, Manou de Madalpour, Bijou, and Djaïpour. They embody the mysterious and enchanting beauty of the breed, a precious heritage in a world where rarity gives it its true value.

Marcel Baudoin-Crevoisier, the undisputed expert in Birmans, praises this extraordinary breed without reservation. He writes with passion:

> *"Let us continue to consider this cat breed as the most beautiful in the world. Its rarity makes it a breed of great value. Due to its mysterious origin, the beauty of its fur, its demeanor, its somewhat enigmatic overall presence, the qualifier 'sacred' given to the Birman cat is not exaggerated."*

Belgium entered the arena in 1932, with *Miss Rousselle*, carrying the Birman heritage to new horizons.

In Switzerland, *Abbé Chamonin* from Geneva, a Persian breeder, joins the dance with Poupée de Rangoon, becoming a key player in Birman breeding in 1933.

Italy is also captivated, with Princess Ratibor Hohenlohe acquiring the majestic *God of Arakan* in 1935.

However, despite this excitement, breeding starts feeling the tremors of the financial crisis of the 1930s. Marcel Baudoin-Crevoisier decides to put an end to his promising breeding, dispersing his precious cats among the most passionate breeders, notably in France, Switzerland, and Italy. In the years leading up to the war, there are few Birmans in exhibitions, and the breed seems to have lost some of its perseverance. The war will deliver a final blow to Birman breeding, leaving only two breeders who will have to revive the breed after the war.

Manou de Madalpour (Photographie de la *Vie à la Campagne*).

BIRMAN: 1930 STANDARD

Appearance, and Size. – The Birman cat, rather small in size, has an elongated body and well-proportioned slender legs. The claws are sharp, curved, strong but fine, and quite brittle. Its weight in adulthood varies between three and four kilograms.

Head. – The head is long with erect ears, covered with white felted fur. The forehead is slightly rounded, the nose slightly snub. The strong lower lip gives the impression of a slightly open mouth. The whiskers are dense and long. The eyebrows are particularly full. The eyes are very mobile, intense royal blue (the sapphire eye of legend), deep, and melancholic. If the animal feels threatened or furious, its gaze becomes fierce, revealing the nature of the little independent wildcat it always aims to be.

Coat – Like all Asian cats, the fur of the Birman cat is long, silky, and of semi-longhair length. The tail hairs are bushy and form a plume less abundant than that of the Angora. Tail – The tail is never short, broken, knotted, or deviated in any way. At first glance, it does not give the impression of the Angora plume: it is thin, not fluffy. It can be compared to the "whip" of Setters in terms of hair nature and appearance. The grip of the tail, thin at the base of the loins, widens. At rest, the tail is carried hanging, slightly curled at the tip. When the animal plays or is furious, the tail stands at a right angle to the body, even turning over on the back in a squirrel plume, bristled, enormous.

Color – The color is, as for the mask, legs, and tail, that of the Siamese with perhaps more bronzed tones on the back. Seen in full sunlight, the coat of the Birman gives the impression of being mixed with threads of burnished gold, hence the name "Gold Cat" given to them by the English who were able to approach them. The four legs give the impression of being clad in otter mittens, with four fingers gloved in white, absolutely pure white up to the first phalanx. The white rises to a point at the back of the hind legs, giving the impression of short-laced boots.

Coat 20
Color and markings 20
Head 15
Eyes 15
Tail 20
Body 10
Total 100

(Ph. Jumaud. Les Races de Chats. 1930.)

BIRMAN: FIFE STANDARD 2016

Size: Medium.

Head: Strong bone structure, slightly rounded forehead, full and slightly rounded cheeks. The nose is of medium length, without a stop, and slightly curved. The chin is firm.

Ears: Fairly small, with rounded tips, well-spaced and slightly inclined, not too straight on the head.

Eyes: Not perfectly round, slightly oval, of medium size. The color is dark blue.

Body: The body structure is quite long. Males are more massive than females.

Limbs: Short and strong, with rounded paws.

Gloving: White paws on the front and hind limbs, called "gloves," are the distinctive feature of the Sacred Birman. These gloves must be absolutely pure white, stopping at the joint or the transition between the toes and the metacarpus without exceeding it. Slightly higher gloves on the hind limbs are tolerated. On the plantar surface of the hind limbs, the white gloves end in points (spurs). Ideal points end in an inverted V between 1/2 and 3/4 of the plantar surface. Points that are slightly higher or lower are acceptable but cannot exceed the joint. It is important that the gloves are of equal length and exhibit symmetrical whiteness between the two front and two hind limbs, and ideally between all four limbs.

Tail: Medium length, feather shaped.

Coat: Long to medium length depending on the body parts. Short on the face, gradually lengthening on the cheeks to form a complete ruff, and long on the back and sides. Silky texture. Some undercoat.

Color: The Sacred Birman exhibits all the characteristics of Siamese pointed cats, but all four paws are white (gloves). Points include the face, ears, limbs, tail, and genital parts. Points should be of uniform color and well-contrasted with the body color. Body color: as described in the general part of the standards, under Siamese Pointed. The color of markings and the body only becomes apparent in adulthood.

Notes: The Sacred Birman has a distinctive and specific morphology for the breed.

Faults: Pure white or colored spots on the chest or belly. Incomplete nose pigmentation. White markings extending from the gloves on the sides or on the undersides of the front or hind limbs (called laces). Absence of spurs on the hind limbs. White spots in colored parts or vice versa. A white spot on the genital parts.

THE BIRMAN ANCESTORS

Manou de Madapour

« DIEU D'ARAKAN » vu de profil. Ce sujet, provenant de croisement, est supérieur au type ordinaire par sa beauté et sa rusticité.

LE MÊME, VU DE FACE, présente une silhouette unique. Admirez sa jolie collerette.

Chat sacré de Birmanie

" DIEU D'ARAKAN ", Champion international à M. Baudoin (C. C. P.).

Un des plus magnifiques parmi les très rares spécimens de cette race mystérieuse actuellement en Europe.

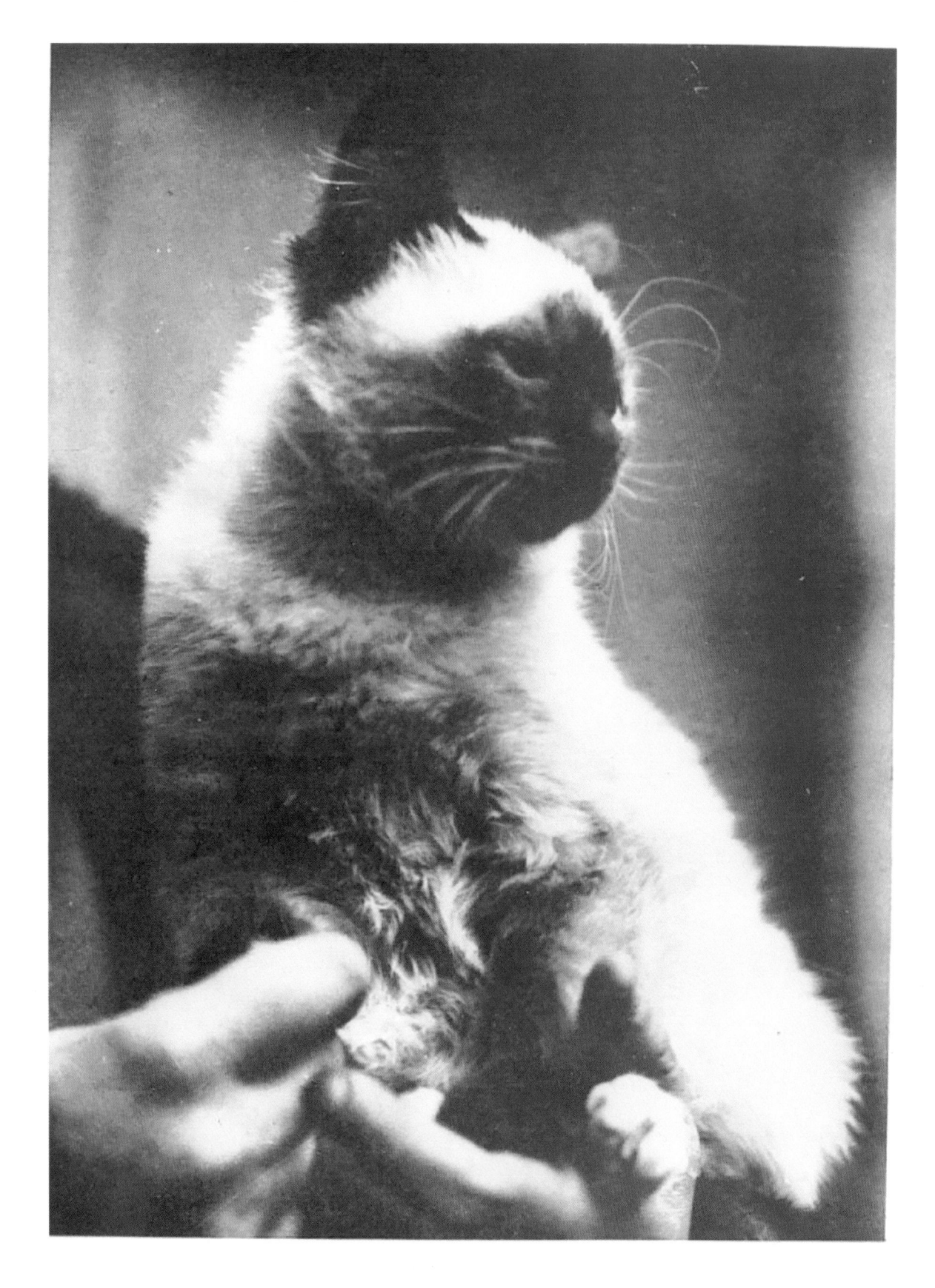

Chatte sacrée de Birmanie
"ZAQUELLE DE MANDALAY" à M. Baudoin, de Saint-Denis (C. C. P.).

Chat de Birmanie.
Hiram, Roi de Madalpour, mâle de 30 mois,
n'atteint que le prix de 3 à 4.000 fr.

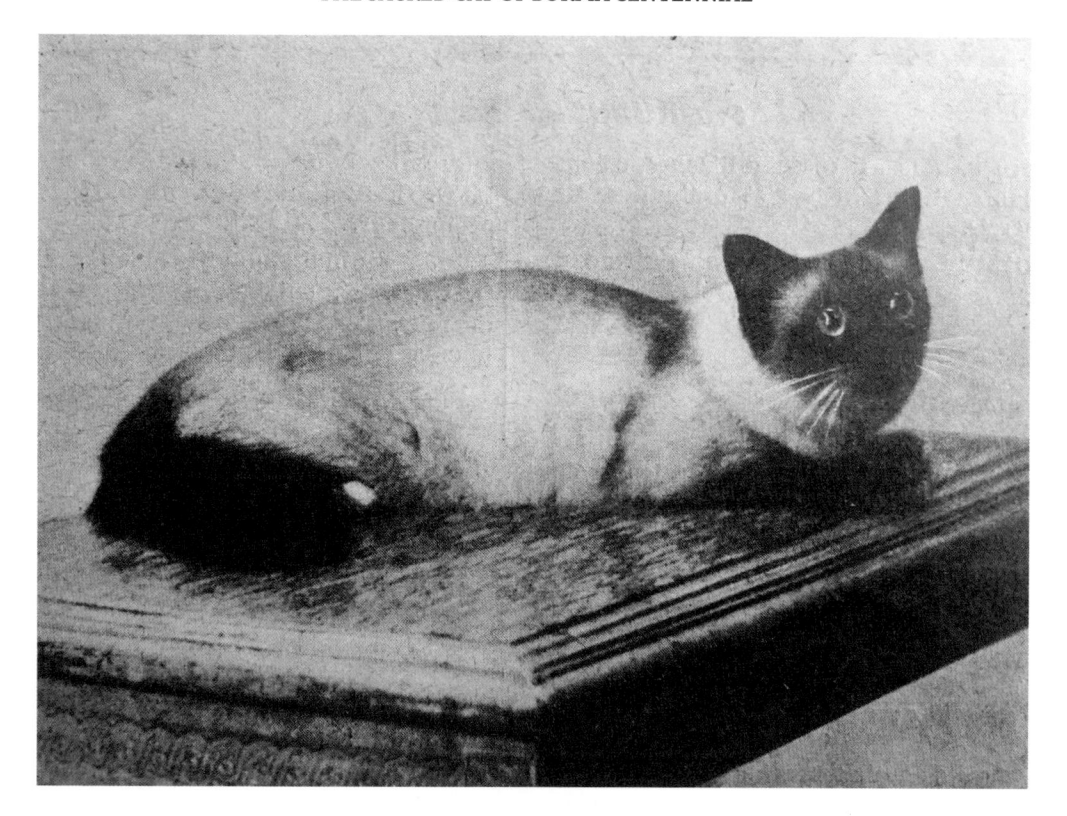

Nafaghi de Madalpour

Chat de Birmanie à Mme Brassart
Lon Saïto de Madalpour

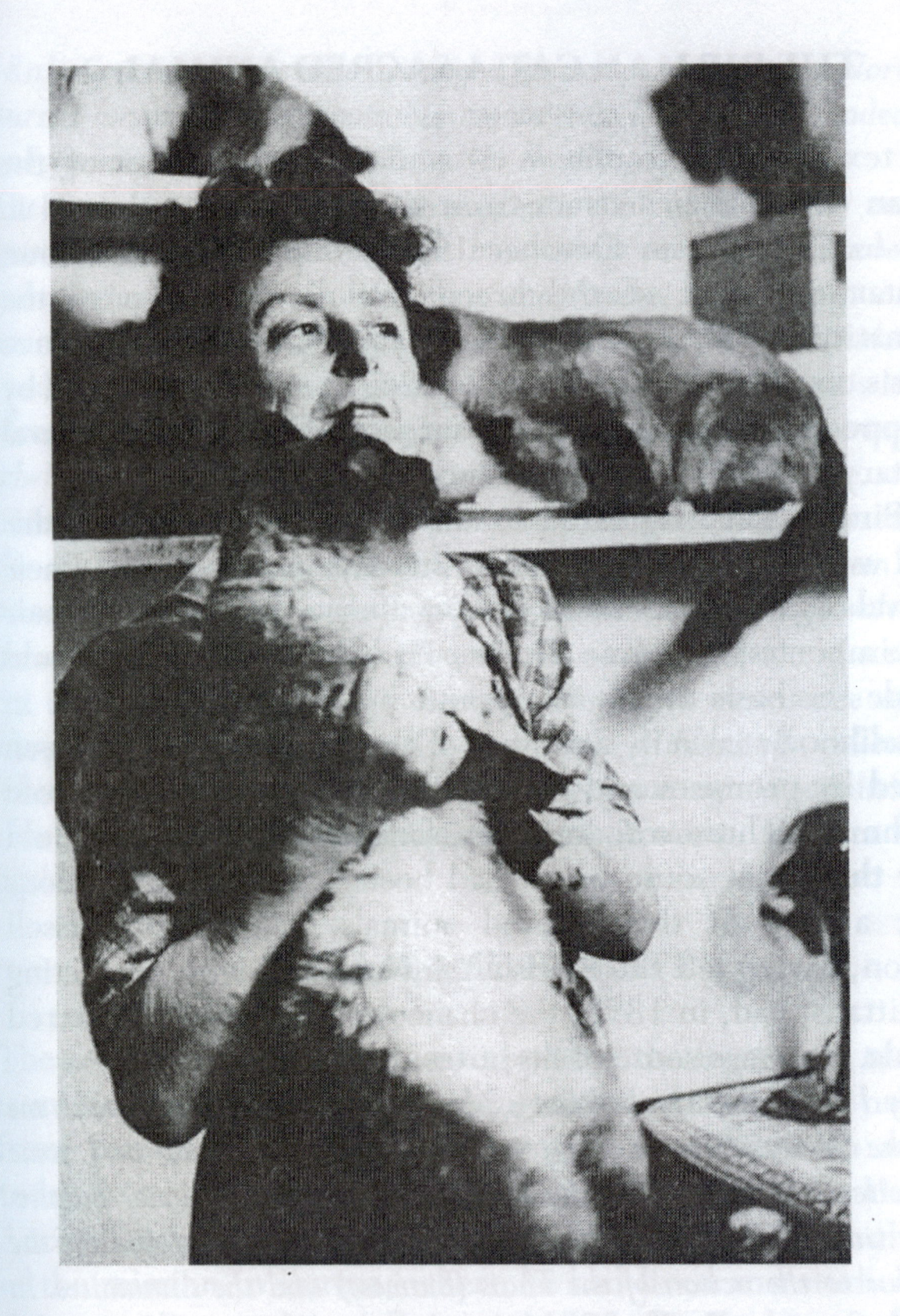

A moving picture, taken at the end of the war 1945: Madeleine Boyer with Orloff de Kaabaa

Djaïpur de Madalpour

CREATION OF COLORS THROUGHOUT THE AGES.

The fascinating history of the evolution of colors in Birmans takes us on a journey through time and the passionate breeding of these elegant felines.

The early Birmans were **Seal-Point**, proudly displaying their black extremities, but according to articles from that time, it seems that chocolate Birmans made their appearance before 1940.

34. Dieu d'Arakhan, *l'un des plus beaux chats sacrés de Birmanie.*

After the tumultuous period of war, pioneering breeders decided to explore new possibilities by introducing the dilution gene to Seal, giving birth to the **Blue-Point.**

In 1955, *Éloi-Eryx de Madalpour*, raised by Mrs. Chaumont-Doisy, became one of the most significant carriers of the blue gene. France was laying the foundation for a new era for Birmans.

Towards the late 1950s, the French cattery "Des Muses" decided to innovate by crossing a Blue Persian named "Bluette de la Côte d'Azur" with Birmans. The result was the creation of the new line of Blue-Point Birmans, with cats like *Iris du Clos Fleuri,* born on August 21, 1959, who dazzled the world of cat shows.

In the United States, another breeding pioneer, Miss Gertrude Griswold, gave birth to one of the first Blue-Points, named "*Griswold's Birman Boi Bleu,*" in 1964. This cat was later bred in Germany under the name "*Ghandi von Assindia*" and then found its place in England with Miss Fisher of the "Praha" cattery.

However, the new colors of the Birman would mainly emerge in the United Kingdom in the 1970s. The strict quarantine rules imposed at the time forced British breeders to work with national resources, giving rise to chocolate and lilac colors.

In 1975, two catteries, *"Shwechinthe"* (owned by Dr. Elizabeth Brigliadori) and *"Mandessa"* (owned by Mrs. Shirley Wilson-Smith), collaborated to introduce these new colors. A lilac-point Persian colorpoint named "Mingchiu Manakini" was used, bringing with it a rich genetic heritage. Thus, in 1976, "Shwechinthe Mandessa," an intermediate blue male carrying the lilac gene, was born.

Mingchui Manakini (Persan Colorpoint Lilac-point)

The following year, the Mandessa cattery used a chocolate Siamese named **Dear Dominic** (born on March 22, 1970) with a Seal-Point Birman named Cragland Darlene to create a seal-point hybrid female: Mandessa Abygail (born on May 11, 1976).

Dear Dominic (Siamese Seal-Point)

This genetic work aims to respect the harmony of the Birman's origins and the systematic work of previous breeders to maintain the original type and characteristics. That is, always using a Persian (colorpoint) on one side and a Siamese on the other. The use of a blue Birman and then a seal Birman also ensures the continuity of Birman lines. This choice also ensures greater genetic diversity of Birman genes, adding two new different genetic lines. Fifty percent of these new cats thus bring a new heritage.

In 1977, these two lines were crossed, obtaining four different colors in July: Seal-Point, Blue-Point, Chocolate-Point, and Lilac-Point. Among this litter and subsequent ones, two female cats carried the desired color: Mandessa Bianca (born on May 30, 1977) and Mandessa Brita (born on July 20, 1977).

Chocolate-Point Creation: F

Persan Lilac-Point	Birman Blue-Point	Siamese Chocolate Point	Birman Seal-Point
Mingchiu Manakini	Ambur Blue Thongwa	Dear Dominic	Cragland Darlene
Blue-point Cat		**Seal-Point Cat**	
Shwechinthe Mandessa (MALE) 08-10-1975		Mandessa Abygail (FEMALE) 05-11-1976	

Chocolate-Point FEMALES
Mandessa Bianca 05-30-1977
Mandessa Brita 07-20-1977

To diversify the lineage, the Shwechinthe cattery also used another combination. A chocolate-point Persian colorpoint named Mingchiu Nobbi (born on July 10, 1975) was also used with another Seal-Point Birman named Cragland Ionne (born on May 30, 1977). With this new combination, they obtained Shwechinthe Aero, a Seal-Point Birman carrying the chocolate gene.

Chocolate-Point Male

Persan Chocolate-point	Birman Seal-Point
Mingchiu Nobbi 07-10-1975	Cragland Ionne 06-02-1972

Seal-Point Cat
Shwechinthe Aero 05-30-1977

From this diversity, the lines were successfully crossed, Mandessa Bianca and Mandessa Brita with Shwechinthe Aero.

Mixing the Lines

Blue-Point X Cat (Factor Lilac)	Seal-Point X Cat (Factor Choc)	Persan Chocolate-Point	Birman Seal-point
Shwechinthe Mandessa (MALE) 08-10-1975	Mandessa Abygail (FEMALE) 05-11-1976	Mingchiu Nobbi	Cragland Ionne

Chocolate-Point Female	Chocolate-Point X Male
Mandessa Bianca 05-30-1977	Shwechinthe Aero 05-30-1977
Mandessa Brita 07-20-1977	

From this combination, the fourth generation emerged:

- On Mandessa Cattery side woth Bianca : Mandessa Coral (born on May 31, 1979).

- On Shwechinthe's side, with Brita : Shwechinte MAieless Coco, Caboma, Topaz and Candice (Lilac).

These cats can be found in the pedigree of chocolate and ilacBirmans.

Shwechinthe Akyab (lilac-point)

Shwechinthe Kybo (chocolate-point)

Shwechinthe Mayo (Chocolate-Point) & Aliny (Lilac-Point)

The next color introduced is the **Red-Point**, its dilution being the Cream-Point, and the Tortoiseshell combinations in females (Seal-Tortie, Blue-Tortie, Chocolate-Tortie, Lilac-Tortie-Point).

Once again, it is in the United Kingdom that these colors will come to light. The Red factor opens new possibilities for the breed, being one of the unique genes that can mix with others (torties).

The first red-points were born at Margaret Richards' Mei Hua cattery: Mei Hua Firefly and Mei Hua Firebird. The series of Red-Points was then transferred to Hilken cattery (Hilary and Ken Clarke). They presented Hikken Red Hercule at the 1982 Cat Show and Hilken Red Arrival at the 1983 Birman Show.

Hilken Red Arrival (Red-PoInt)

To obtain individuals of this new color, the Mei Hua cattery used a male Blue-Point Birman named Sahra Soleil Bleu (born on May 7, 1974 – grandson of Ghandi von Assindia) and a hybrid female named Larissa. Larissa was a short-haired hybrid cat, Seal-Tortie, whose father was Ginger Suffolk, a short-haired red-tabby, and the mother was a Seal-Point Birman named Mei-Hua Jocasta. This combination gave birth to two male red-point cats: Mei Hua Firefly and Firebird (born on May 3, 1975). Unfortunately, these lines did not survive in the United Kingdom, fading out after two generations.

It was necessary to start over from scratch in the United Kingdom and create two new lines.

1. **On the MALE side**:

In 1978, the Clarks (Hilken) Stared again with the new prototype cat *Ginger Suffolk*, which produces a short-haired red and white hybrid cat with white-gloved paws, from an unknown mother : *Red-Dawn* (born on June 5, 1978). She was then crossed with a seal-point Birman to give birth t teh fanos *Champion Dematin*.

Red Dawn (June 5, 1978)

Chanson dematin (Seal-Point Male)

From this union, a long-haired male named Hilken Red Venture was born in 1979. He was crossed with a female seal-point Birman named Patrioona Fabia, resulting in the birth of a female Red-Point named Hilken Red Peril (born on October 22, 1980). Utilizing her grandfather Chanson once again, Hilken Red Peril was crossed with him, giving birth to a Seal-Tortie female named Hilken Red Desire (born on September 29, 1981), who later became the mother of Hilken Red Arrival (red-tabby-point male). In 1982, she also gave birth to Hilken Red Hercules (born on May 9, 1982).

Hilken Red Venture (1979)

Hilken Red Hercules (Red-Point - 1982)

2. On the FEMALE side:

From the crossbreeding of *Red-Dawn* and *Chanson Dematin*, a female Seal-Tortie Birman named *Hilken Red Poppy* was born on September 19, 1979. She, too, was later crossed with her father, *Chanson Dematin*, giving rise to a Seal-Tortie female named *Hilken Red Progress*, born on August

24, 1981.

Hilken Red Poppy (19 September 1979)

Hilken Red Progress (Seal-Tortie Point)

Crossing the two lines, *Hilken Red Hercules* (male) with *Hilken Red Progress* (female) resulted in four kittens born on July 29, 1983: Hilken Jason (m), Hilken Red Gamboller (f), Hilken Red Goddess (f), and *Hilken Red Goliath* (m).

Hilken Red Goliath (Red-Point - 1983)

The first exports of the Red lines began in 1984. In Sweden, *Trollehöjds* cattery imported a Red Tabby female named Hilken Cream Debutante (born on October 29, 1984) and crossed this new line with a Seal-Point Birman named Trollehöjds Herkules. The cats produced became part of Swedish pedigrees.

Trollehöjds Herkules (Seal-Point)

In France, Mrs. Marie-Anne Taranger (Srinagar cattery) was the first to import Red-Points from the UK in 1984. These were descendants of Hilken Red Arrival crossed with Hilken Red Cherry of Srinagar. Meanwhile, in Germany, German breeders embarked on the Red-Point task as early as 1972-73.

Rococo Schloss created a Red-Point from a Cream Persian male named Enrico von Assindia. This male was crossed with a Red-Point Birman female of unknown origin named Julia von Rococo Assindia. She produced a long-haired male named Igor von Rococo Schloss. Igor was then crossed with a Seal-Point Birman named Carina von Rococo Schloss, who gave birth to the foundation Seal-Tortie-Point female named Bianca von Rococo Schloss. Bianca produced numerous kittens, including International Champion Smokeyhill Kwang Lie (born on August 20, 1975). Notably, the

Seal-Tortie cat Tonia von Rococo Schloss, and with a Red-Point Birman from the same lineage named Claudius von Rococo Schloss, she produced a male named Jo-Jo von Rococo Schloss. Together, they produced a Seal-Tortie female named Action von Rococo Schloss, forming the basis of the Red lineage at Las Perlas Sin cattery (owned by Mrs. Anneli Falk, later continued by her daughter, Mrs. Bettina Suvi Rode) between 1986 and 1991.

German Red-Point Birman

Persian Cream	Red-point Birman	Blue-Point Birman	Seal-Point Birman
Enrico von Assindia	Julia von Rococo Schloss	Krischan von Assindia	Graziella von Fillmill

Long Hair cat – Red (m)	Seal-Point Birman
Igor von Rococo Schloss	Carina von Rococo Schloss

Seal-Tortie-Point Birman (f)
Bianca von Rococo Schloss

Crossing the Lines: Action

Seal-Tortie-Point Birman	Seal-Point Birman
	a. Smokeyhill Kwang Lie
Bianca von Rococo Schloss (f)	Cream-Point Birman
	b. Claudius von rococo Schloss

Seal-Tortie-Point Birman (f)
a. Tonia von Rococo Schloss
Cream-Point Birman (m)
b. Jo-Jo von Rococo Schloss

Cream-Point Birman	Seal-Tortie-Point Birman
a. Jo-Jo von Rococo Schloss	b. Tonia von Rococo Schloss

Seal-Tortie-Point Birman
Action von Rococo Schloss

The next color gene is Tabby (or Agouti gene), which can mix with all other colors.

We return to Germany with the Las Perlas-Sin cattery for the first attempts to create Tabby colors.

The work for this color began in 1984-86. Mrs. Anneli Falk starts with her Chinchilla Persian female named Mount Badger Chinchin Fleur (1979) and crosses her with a Seal-Point Birman male named Sariak Ch'en Chi Mai (born on May 2, 1980). The result is a hybrid cat named Las-Perlas-Sin Ondine (born on March 29, 1986). This female is then crossed with a Blue-Point Birman named Sofie's Aristocat (born on March 26, 1983). From this union comes the spectacular International Champion Las Perlas-Sin Cepetto, a Seal-Tabby-Point male (born on March 29, 1986) found in most Tabby pedigrees today. The Tabby color is officially recognized by Fife in 1990.

Las Perlas-Sin Cepetto (Seal-Tabby-Point - March 29, 1986)

The next and last color officially recognized is **Silver** and its dilution, **Smoke,** which can also combine with all other colors.

In France, Mrs. Catherine Viltange uses a Black Silver Shaded Persian in 1988, crossing it with a Birman. After years of diligent work, in 1991, she obtains a Seal Tabby Point Birman: First Tabby de Shweli-Sitang, from Daphné de Shweli-Sitang and European Champion Ukar de Samsara. In 1992, she produces her first Seal-Smoke-Point Birman: Himalaya de Shweli-Sitang, who becomes Euro-Champion in 1996, created from a hybrid female, Fleole de Shweli-Sitang, and GIC Chaudron Magique de la Renoué of Hameau Kertweed.

In the 1990s, also in France, Mrs. Geneviève Basquine of the Chatterie des Moulins de Busset decides to work on the new Silver color. She uses a Seal-Silver-Tabby Persian named Fair Play de la Sente aux Eglantiers, crossing it with a Seal-Point Birman named Douchka de Habenera (carrying the chocolate factor). She obtains a hybrid Chocolate-Silver-Point female named Gipsy des Moulin de Busset. From this female, she works with the German line, with a Tabby descendant of Cepetto Las Perlas-Sin named Eros des Moulins de Busset, producing one of the first Seal-Silver Tabby Birmans, named Helios Sun Shine des Moulins de Busset. By crossing this male with her female Erys des Moulins de Busset (Blue-Tabby), she obtains the magnificent **Leonidas des Moulins de Busset**, a Seal-Silver-Tabby male found in many modern pedigrees.

Leonidas des Moulins de Busset

Seal-Silver-Tabby-Point

Persan Seal-Silver-Tabby	Seal-Point Birman	Seal-Tabby Birman	Seal-Point Birman
Fair Play de la Sente aux Églantiers	Douchka de Habanera	Cepetto Las Perlas-Sin	Carmen con de Kaaij
Chocolate-Silver-Tabby Long Hair		**Seal-Tabby Birman**	
Gipsy des Moulins de Busset		Eros des Moulins de Busset	
	Seal-Silver-Tabby Birman	**Blue-Tabby Birman**	
	Helios Sun Shine des Moulins de Busset	Erys du Moulin des Bussets	
	Seal-Silver-Tabby-Point Birman		
	Leonidas du Moulin du Busset		

Another breeder in Switzerland, Mme Josette Savary (Saya San cattery) did the same work in 1994. She also used a Persian chinchilla, Fantasia de Semiramis, crossed with a chocolate-point Birman, Shwechinthe Nefos (04-09-1993). The female produced was a long hair silver cat, Hadji de Saya San. She wed this female with a seal-tabby-point Birman, Bou d'Chou de la Thur and, from this union Markus de Saya San was born (04-24-1996) -chocolate carrier-, a seal-silver-tabby male and a Seal Smoke, Macadam de Saya San.

Meanwhile, another French cattery, Sacré Roi (Jean-Luc Odeyer), in South of France, became interested in the new "pastel" colors. After acquiring the silver lines from des Moulins de Musset et de Saya San, he decided to work on the chocolate-silver-tabby color, smoke lines and tortie-silver introducing the red gene in this pool. He created Nickel Chrome du Sacré Roi, a chocolate smoke male with his seal-point Birman, Lolita Brin d'amour du Sacré Roi.

Mr. Odeyer works also since 2010 on the new colors: The Cinnamon and the fawn point. In order to do so, he used a British shorthair fawn point female, **Babayaga du Chêne Landry**, and a female cinnamon tortie-point, **Rosa Majalis**.

In New Zeeland. the cattery of Rakesha is also working on these new colors.

BIRMAN GENETIC: COLORS

This chapter will help you understand color tests conducted by veterinary laboratories (such as UC Davis, for example).

The term used to designate the precise location of a particular gene on the chromosome carrying it is LOCUS. Genes are DNA fragments stored in the cell nucleus, containing instructions for specialized protein production. All cells in an individual (except gametes) have the same set of genes.

Alleles are the different forms a gene can take, occupying a specific location on a chromosome. Birman color genes can be divided into four categories:

1. **Fundamental color genes:** Include Colorpoint (Locus C), Agouti (Locus A), Orange (Locus O), and Amber (Locus E).
2. **Modification genes for fundamental colors:** Include Brown (Locus B), Dilution (Locus D), as well as Dilution Modification Locus (Locus Dm) and Silver (Inhibitor, I Locus).
3. **Color variation genes:** Include Tabby and Ticked. This group of genes pigments hairs and can create variable stripes, giving fur a distinct appearance.
4. **White gloves gene for Birman (Locus G) (G = gloves).**

Genes are always associated in pairs. A gene can be dominant (only one is needed) or recessive (two are needed).

1. Fundamental color genes:

Color is created by melanin pigments in hair, skin, and eyes. The two fundamental pigments are **black** *(eumelanin)* and yellow *(pheomelanin)*. An individual hair can be either entirely black, entirely yellow, or a mix of black and yellow.

Colorpoint and Locus C:

Locus C is a dominant gene for **pigmentation.** When active, it produces black or orange pigments throughout the body. A recessive mutation of this gene results in white color. The colorpoint mutation has a unique effect: ears, paws, and tail retain pigmented colors while the body remains clear. Several cat breeds have this specific locus: Siamese and Birman, notably. This gene is written as **Cs** (s = Siamese). The temperature of the body is linked to this difference. The colder extremities retain color, while the warmer body stays clear. It's a recessive gene, so to express it, it must be on both genes: cs/cs.

Agouti gene and Locus A:

The **Agouti** gene on **Locus A** is central for yellow pigmentation. This gene can be active (yellow pigment can appear) or inactive (prevents yellow formation but allows black gene manifestation). A normal Agouti gene is dominant, allowing the cat to present yellow and black stripes on its fur, allowing TABBY genes to express (see below). A recessive mutation of Locus A allows the cat to have a solid color. A cat with black coloring is then called **SEAL**. This mutation prevents Tabby genes from manifesting. It's said that the cat is a/a (non-agouti). Agouti is sometimes called Lynx. If the cat is A, it's Agouti, yellow in stripes, and it allows the appearance of Tabby and Smoke genes.

Orange and Locus O:

The Orange gene **(Locus O)** gives a red/orange color to the fur. Cats are the only ones with this gene, found only on the X chromosome, so it's more sex-specific (Cats and humans have two pairs of sex-linked chromosomes: X = female, Y = male. A female is XX, and a male is XY). There are two versions of this gene: the dominant Orange allele O and the recessive non-orange allele o. The O pigment blocks the black pigment (eumelanin) and only allows the manifestation of the yellow pigment (pheomelanin). The o allele, however, allows the manifestation of both black and orange. As female cats have two X chromosomes (XX), four options present themselves: OO = the cat is Orange/Red, oo = the cat is Black (or another color), Oo or oO = the cat is a mix of orange and black (or another color). This is called Tortie. Since a male is XY, he can be either Orange or Seal (or another color).

Orange Allele Blocking Agouti Gene (Locus A):

The **dominant O allele** also blocks the Agouti gene (Locus A), thus preventing the formation of tabby genes. However, this is not absolute, and traces of tabby can be observed on the legs, tail, and face.

Locus E, Amber:

The **Locus E** is also called Extension. This gene, to our knowledge, is not crucial for the Birman. It is linked to the production of black pigment and the Amber color.

2. Modification Genes for Basic Colors:

These genes do not produce color pigments but influence color by reducing their intensity. These modifier genes include **Brown (Locus B)**, **Dilution (Locus D)**, Dilution Modifier (Locus D-M), and Silver (Locus I, Inhibitor).

Brown and Locus B:

The **Brown gene (Locus B** = full color) influences the intensity of black pigment. It is a recessive gene, so it must appear on both genes to manifest. It can give rise to brown, called **Chocolate (bb)**, or if diluted once more, to **Cinnamon (b'b')**.

- A Bb cat will be Seal/Black.
- A bb cat will be Chocolate.
- A b'b' cat will be Cinnamon.

Dilution and Locus D:

The **Dilution gene D** modifies colors by washing or diluting black and orange pigments. This gene is recessive and must be present on both genes to manifest (dd).

- A black cat (Seal - B/) becomes gray (Blue). Genes are B/dd.
- A Chocolate cat (bb) becomes Lilac. Genes are bb/dd.
- A Cinnamon cat (b'b') becomes Fawn (Sable). Genes are b'b'/dd.
- An Orange cat (OO) becomes cream. Genes are OO/dd.

A cat with a dominant gene can also be a carrier of the dilution gene without it manifesting. It may appear in their offspring if the partner is also a carrier of the dilution gene.

- Bd = Seal carrier of dilution
- bd = Chocolate carrier of dilution
- b'd = Cinnamon carrier of dilution

Dilution Modifier Gene (Dm):

There is also a dominant **dilution modifier gene (Dm)** that can act on diluted colors (dd).

- A Blue (B/dd) can be diluted into a Blue-Caramel (Dm).
- A Lilac (bb/dd) can be diluted into a Lilac-Caramel (Dm).
- A Fawn (b'b'/dd) can be diluted into a Sable-Caramel (Dm).
- A Cream (OO/dd) can be diluted into an Apricot (Dm).

Silver (Inhibitor, Locus I):

The silver/argent gene somewhat suppresses melanin production and yellow pigment production. For tabby cats, the base color of the fur becomes pale or "silver," resulting in a Silver-Tabby. For solid-colored cats, the base of the fur becomes pale, creating a color called Silver-Smoke.

3. White Spots (Locus S) and Gloves (Locus G):

Locus S is responsible for white spots in the fur. It's not entirely clear if there is one or more loci. For the Birman, the presence of Locus G (gloves) has been detected, responsible for the gloves. To have a gloved cat, the gene must be on the pair (GG) because it is a recessive gene. It is a mutation of the white gene.

4. Genes for Color Patterns:

Tabby is a fur pattern in domestic cats (purebred and mixed breed) that presents an agouti pattern composed of alternating dark and light color bands along the hair shaft with contrasting darker spots, stripes, or swirls and a prominent "M" on the forehead.

Tabby colors (**Ta**) result from combinations of basic black and yellow colors between hair groups and even within a single hair. Several genes are involved. The tabby coat requires a functional Agouti gene (A), which is masked in a black cat (aa). They can also cover other basic colors. There are three genes associated with these patterns: mackerel (striped) and classic (marbled) tabby, ticked tabby, and spotted tabby. It is a dominant gene found in all aforementioned colors. The Birman falls into the classic tabby and ticked (silver-tabby) classes.
In addition to these color genes, the Birman also possesses the Longhair gene (LL).

Example Test: ULTIMATUM of LADDAK Conducted by UC Davis

COAT COLOR TEST REPORT

UC DAVIS VETERINARY MEDICINE
Veterinary Genetics Laboratory

Provided Information:

Name:	ULTIMATUM
Registration:	2182-03027537

Case:	CAT148070
Date Received:	04-Dec-2023
Report Issue Date:	06-Dec-2023
Report ID:	9522-6416-5918-0095

Verify report at www.vgl.ucdavis.edu/verify

DOB: 08/16/2023 **Sex:** Male **Breed:** Birman **Color:** seal-point ?

Sire:	DU MANOIR D'AMBRE TÉLÉMAQUE	Dam:	CH DU LADDAK SAMANTHA	
Reg:	0082-02995373	Reg:	2149-02944870	
Microchip:		Microchip:		

RESULT		INTERPRETATION
AGOUTI	a/a	Non-agouti. If bred to a non-agouti, only non-agouti offspring will be produced.
ALBINO		Not requested.
AMBER	E/E	No copies of the mutation for Amber.
BROWN	B/b	Full color, carrier of brown.
COLORPOINT	c^s/c^s	Siamese.
DILUTE	D/d	One copy of dilute allele. Cat is a carrier of dilute.
DOMINANT WHITE & WHITE SPOTTING		Not requested.
GLOVES	G/G	Two copies of Birman gloving mutation are present.

Test Result:

Ultimatum is a/a, therefore not Agouti (no Tabby); E/E, so no Amber mutation; Bb, thus he is SEAL but carries the *chocolate* color gene; CsCs, therefore Colorpoint; D/d, so he is **SEAL** but carries the *dilution* gene; G/G, thus he has *white gloves*.

Ultimatum is a Gloved Seal-Point, carrying chocolate and dilution genes.

THE CENTENNIAL PICTURES

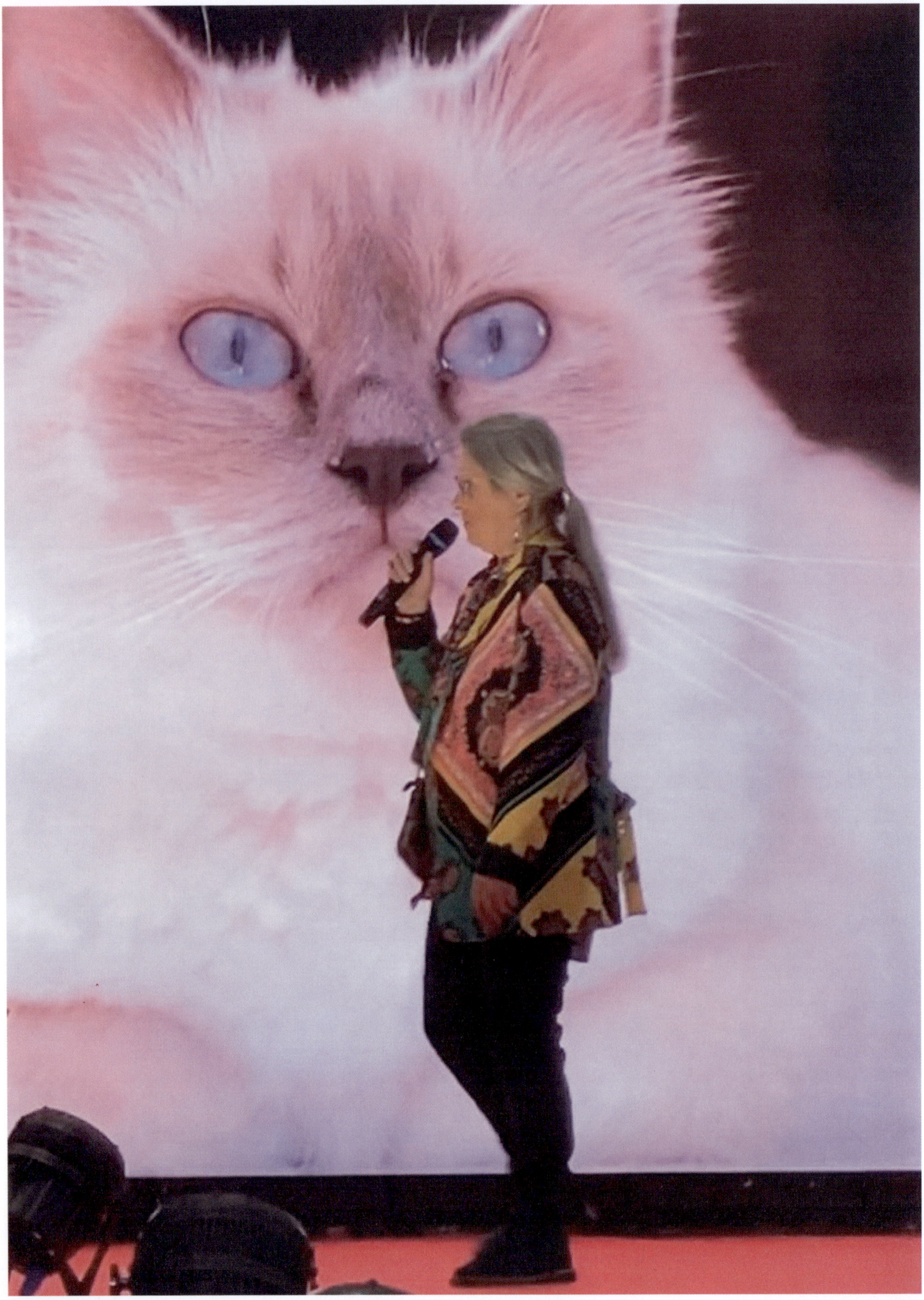

THE SACRED CAT OF BURMA CENTENNIAL

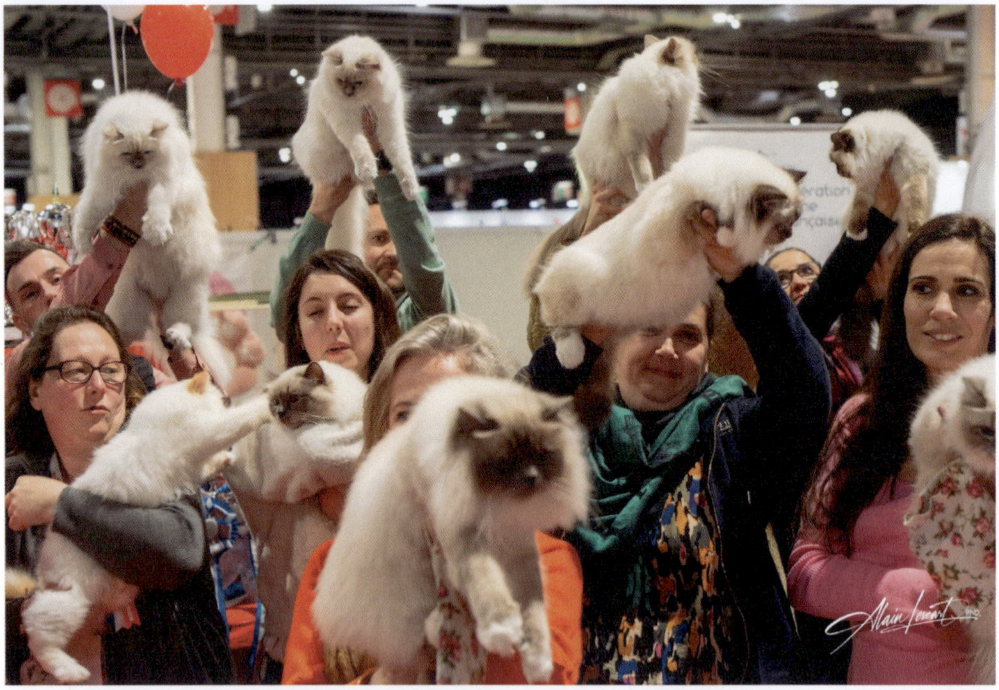
Alain Lescart PhD.

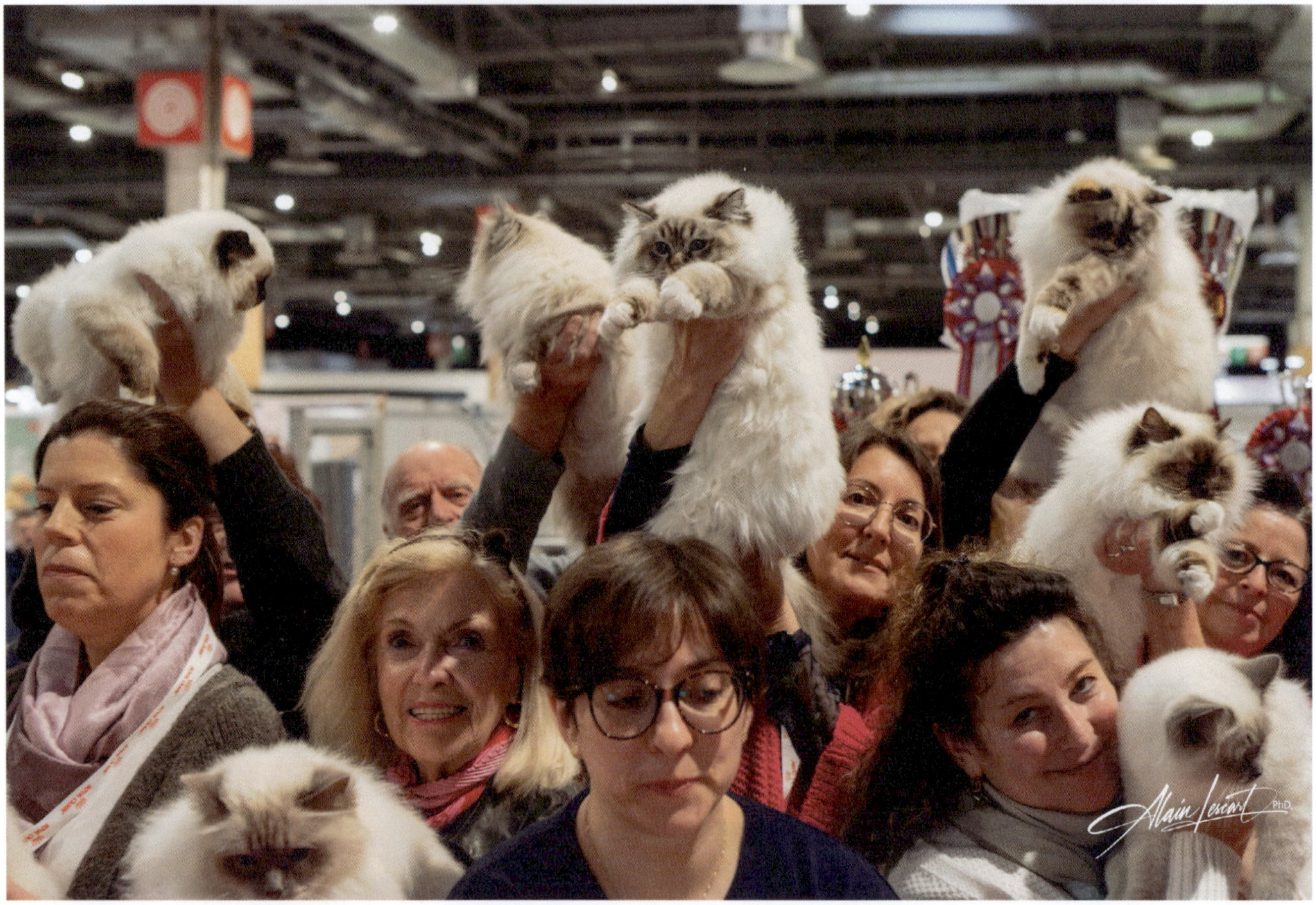
Alain Lescart PhD.

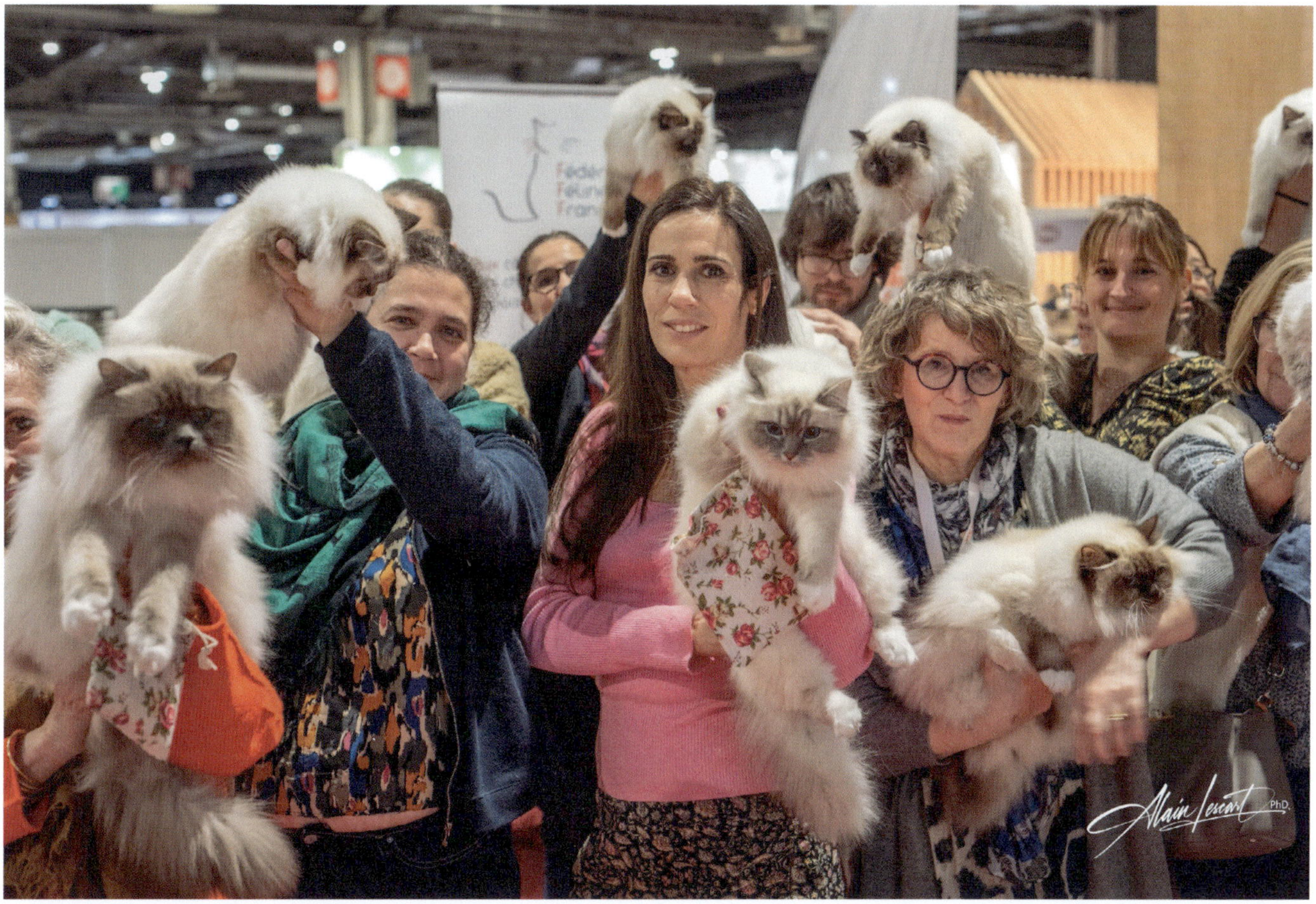

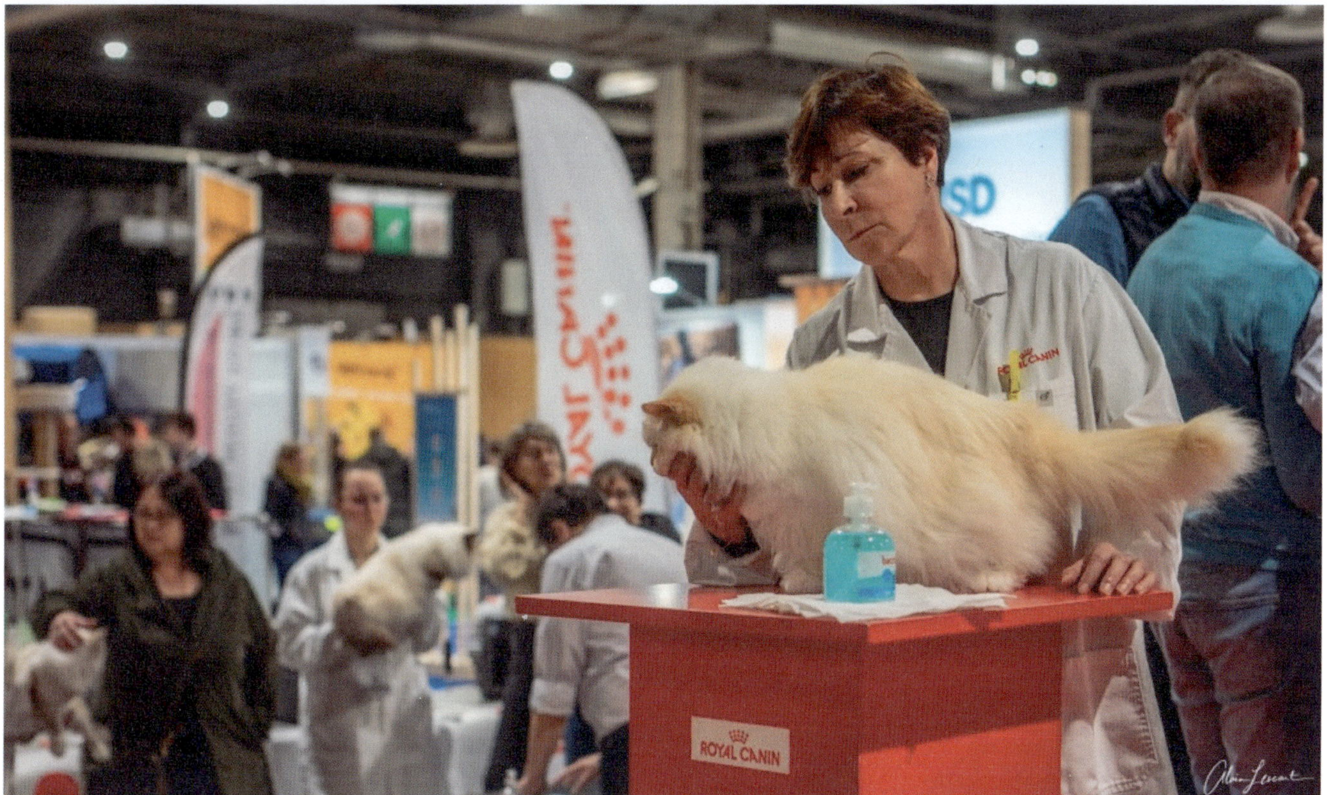
ROYAL CANIN

ALAIN LESCART

THE SACRED CAT OF BURMA CENTENNIAL

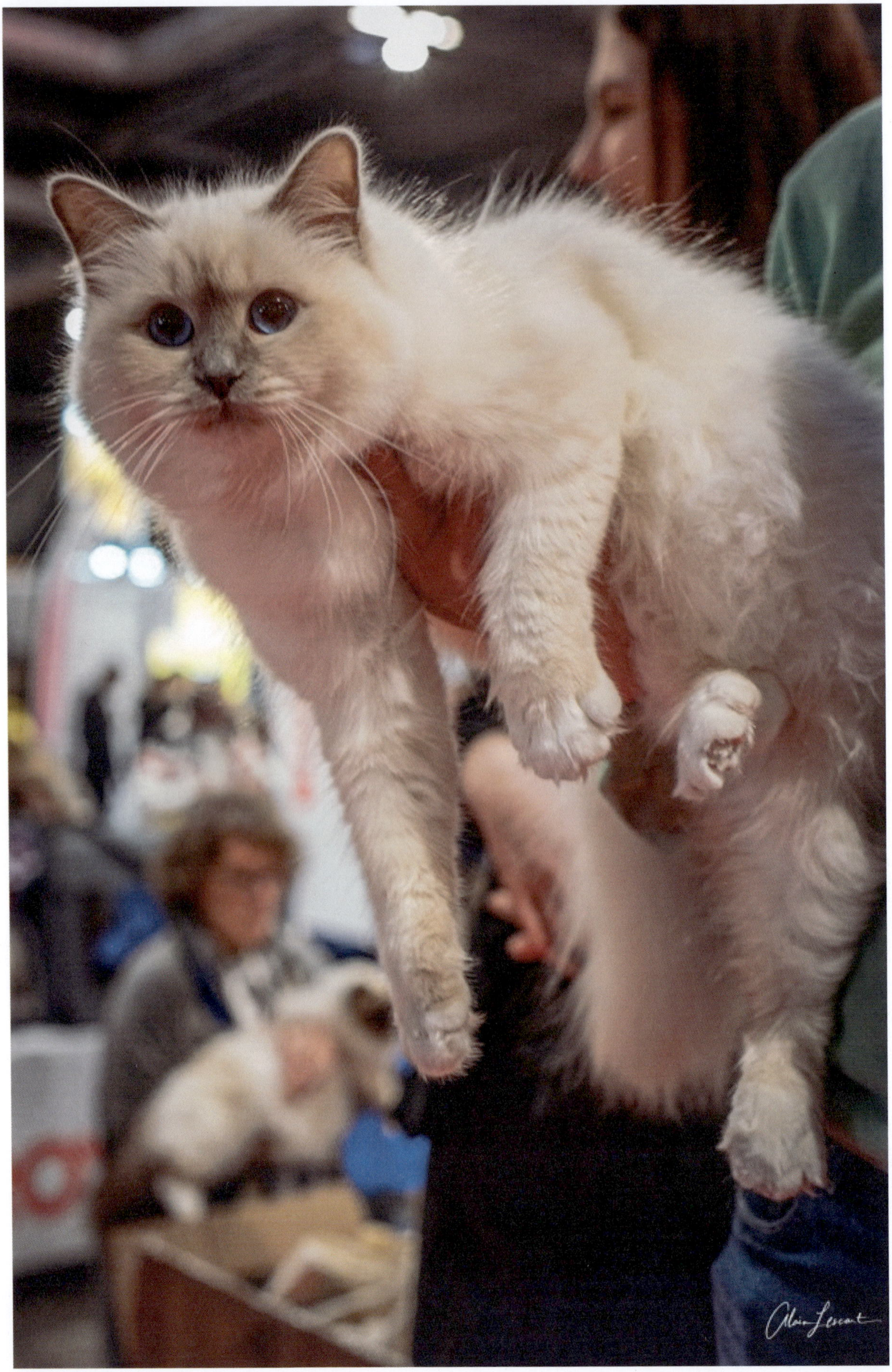

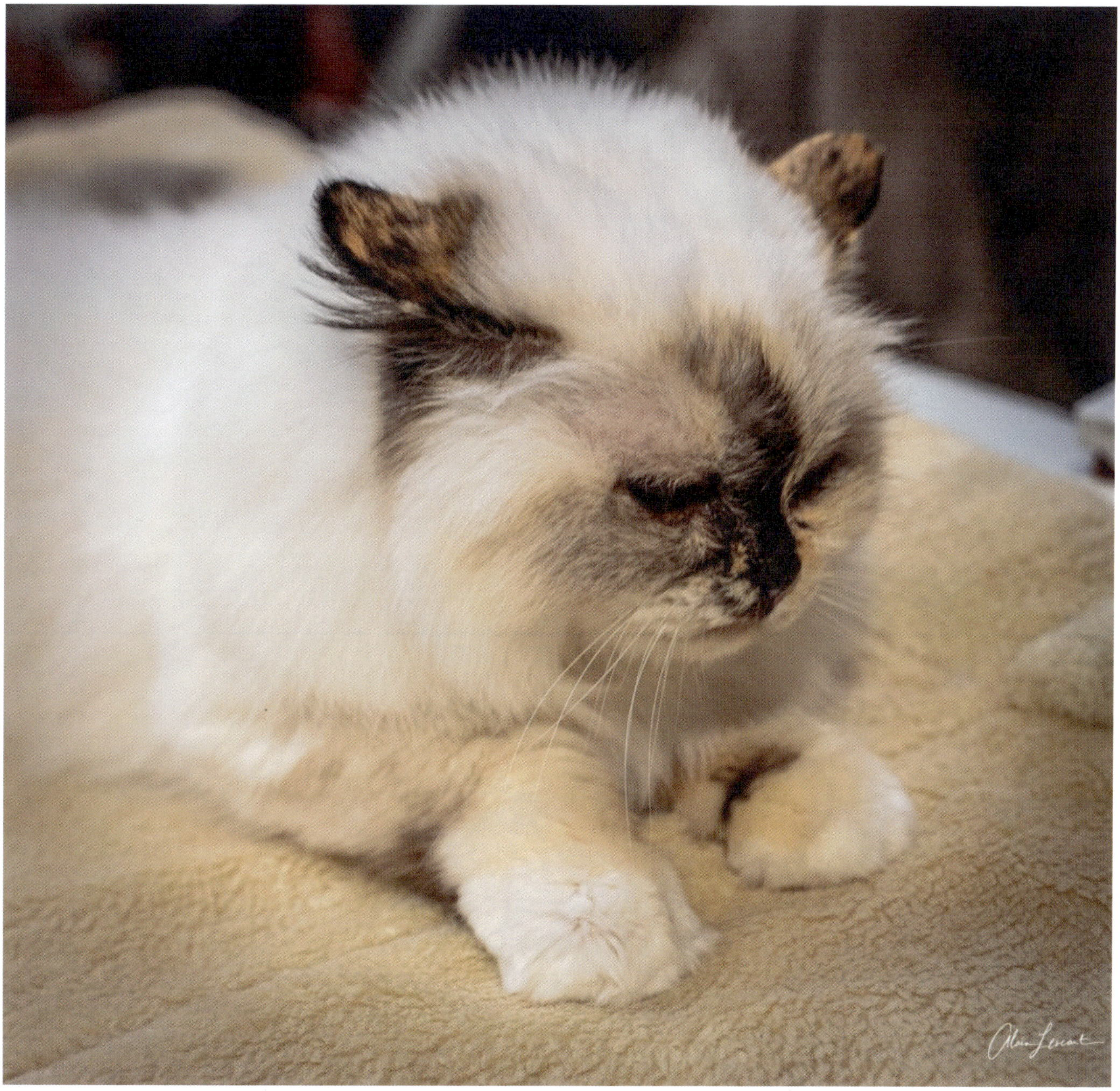

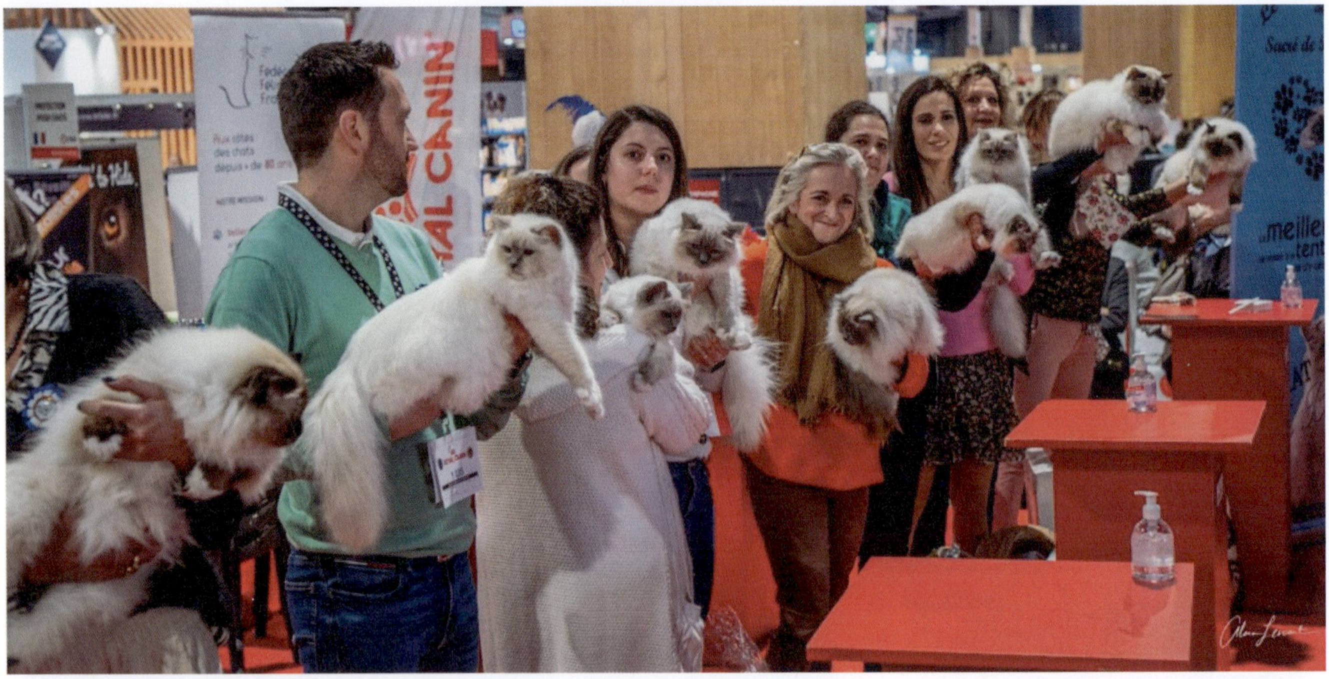
AL CANIN

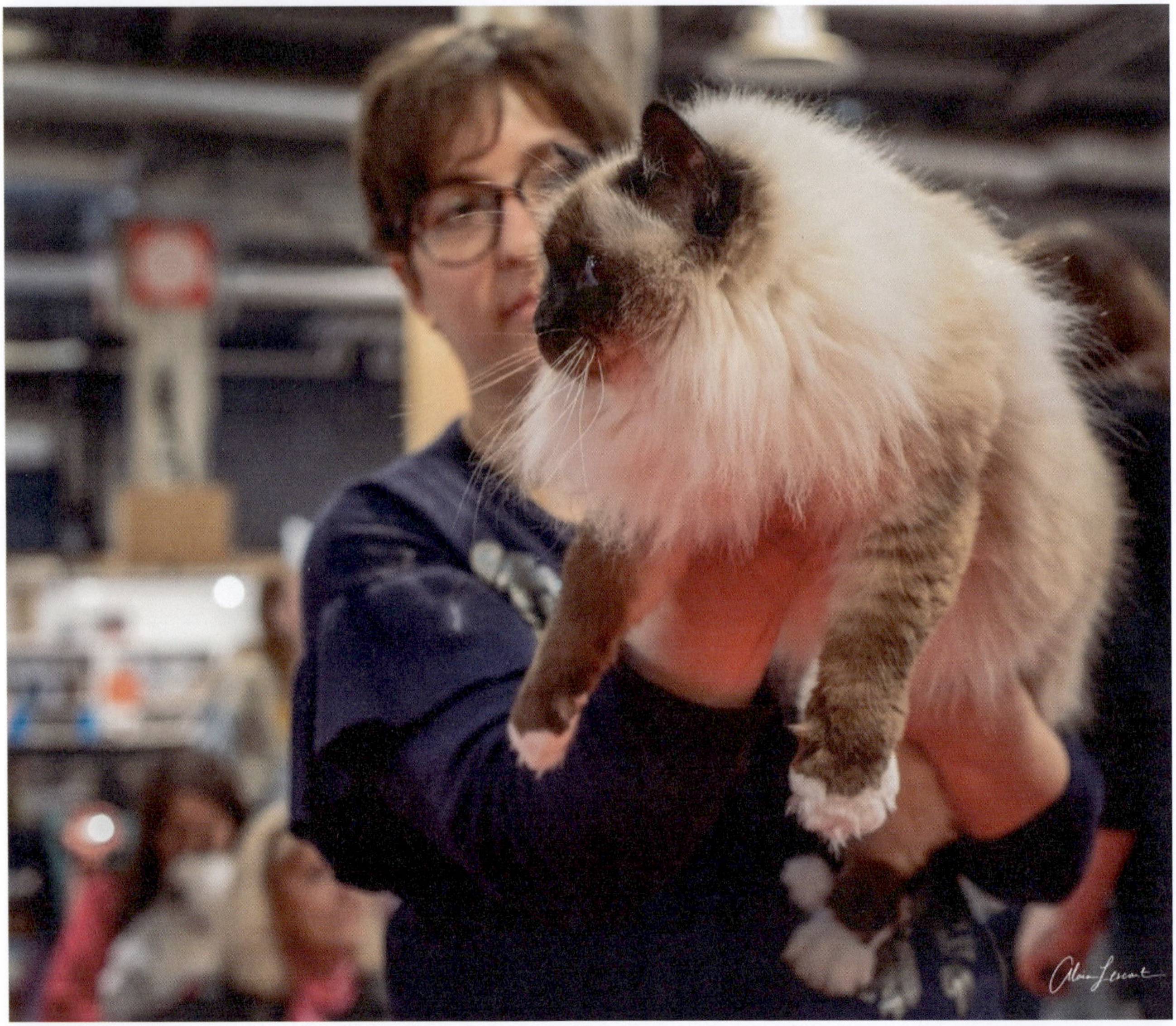
Alain Lescart

THE SACRED CAT OF BURMA CENTENNIAL

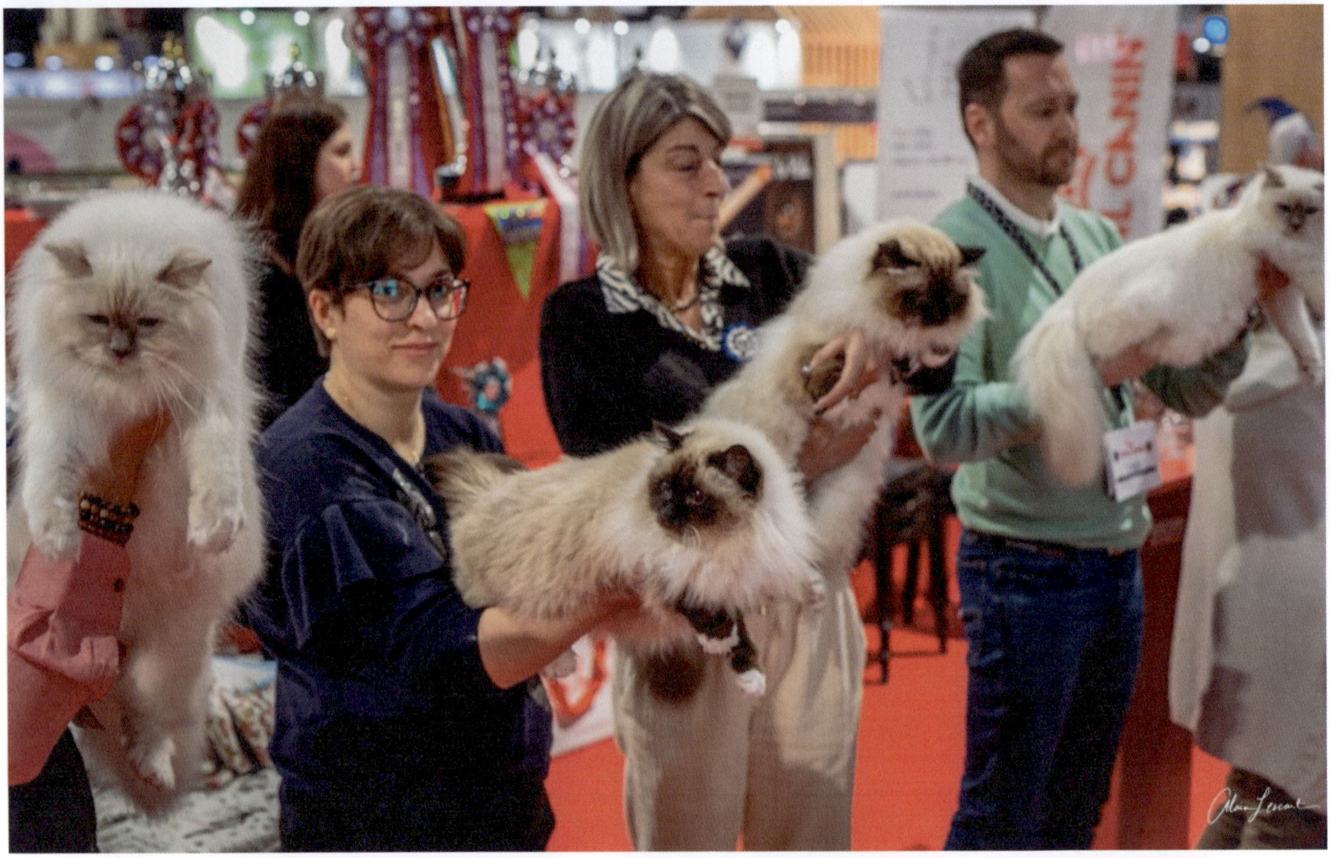
Alain Lescart

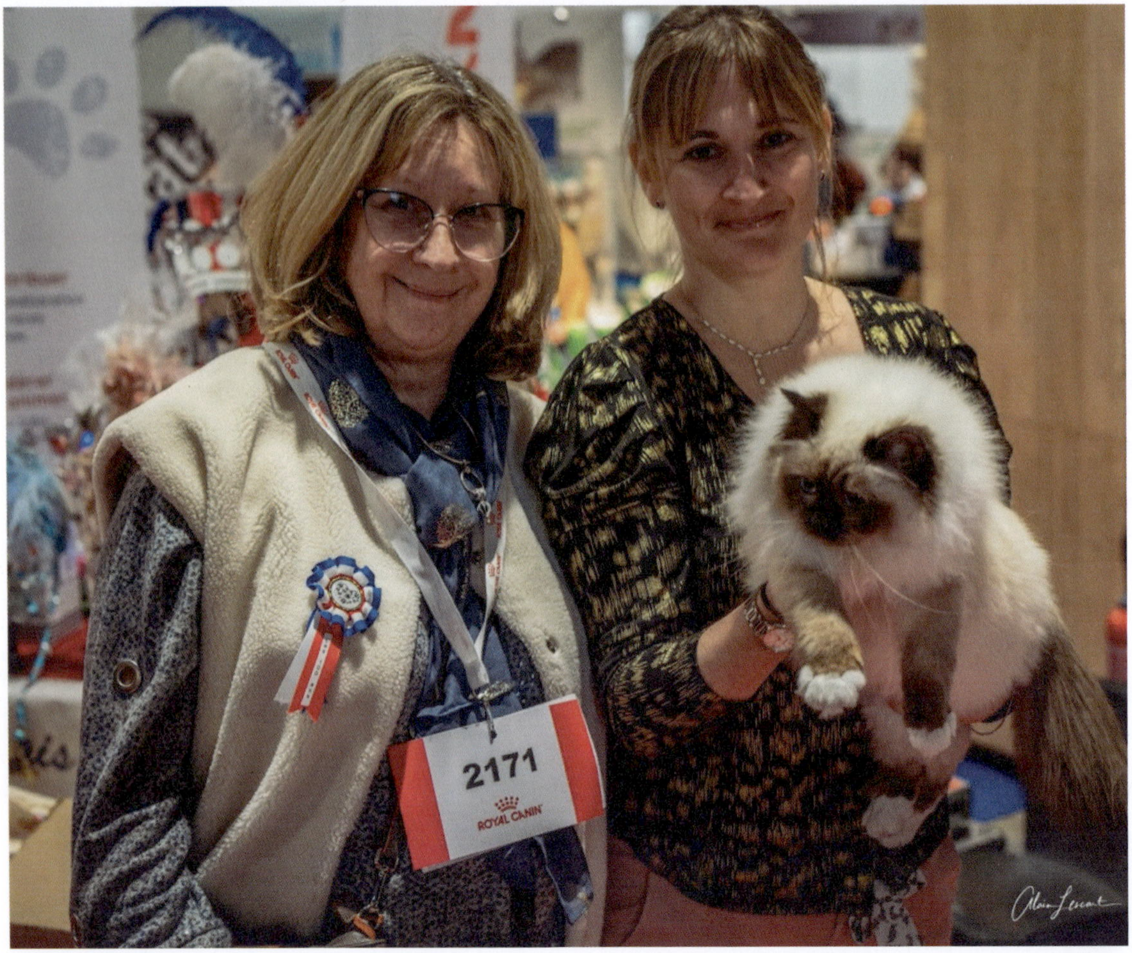
2171
ROYAL CANIN
Alain Lescart

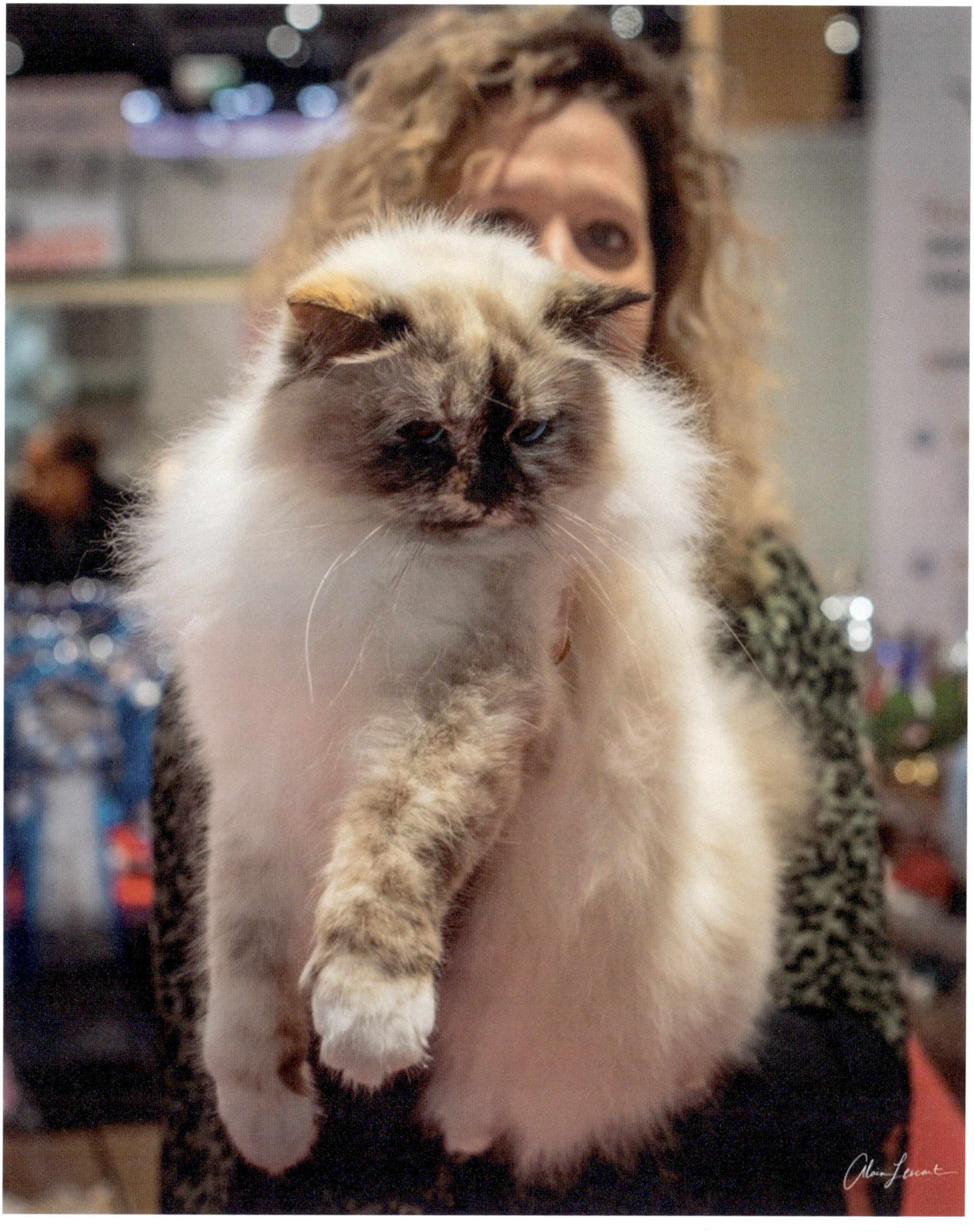

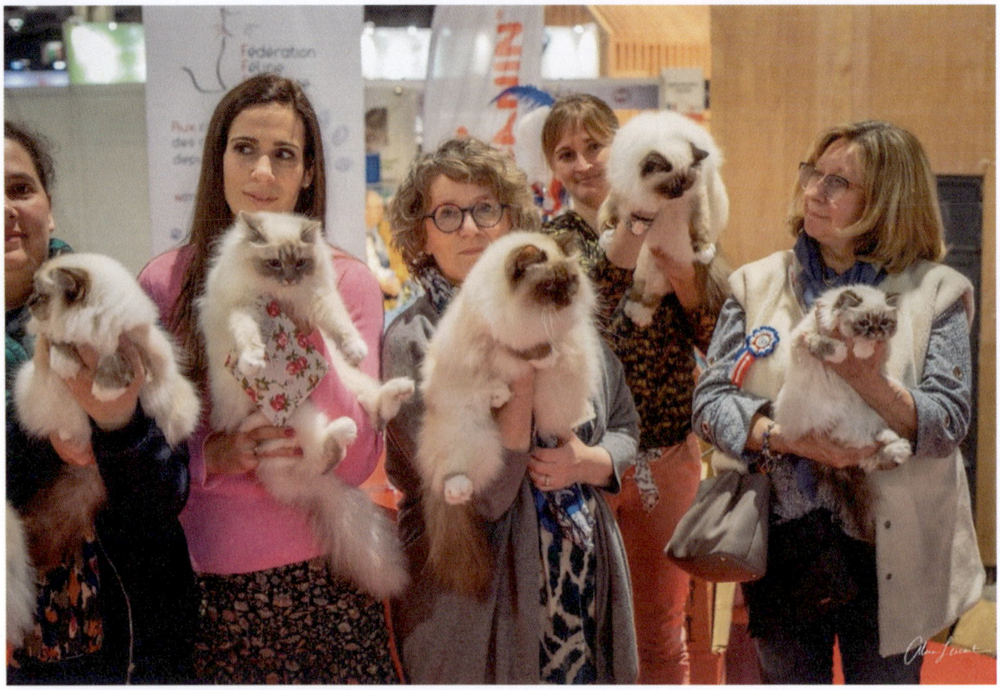
Fédération
Féline

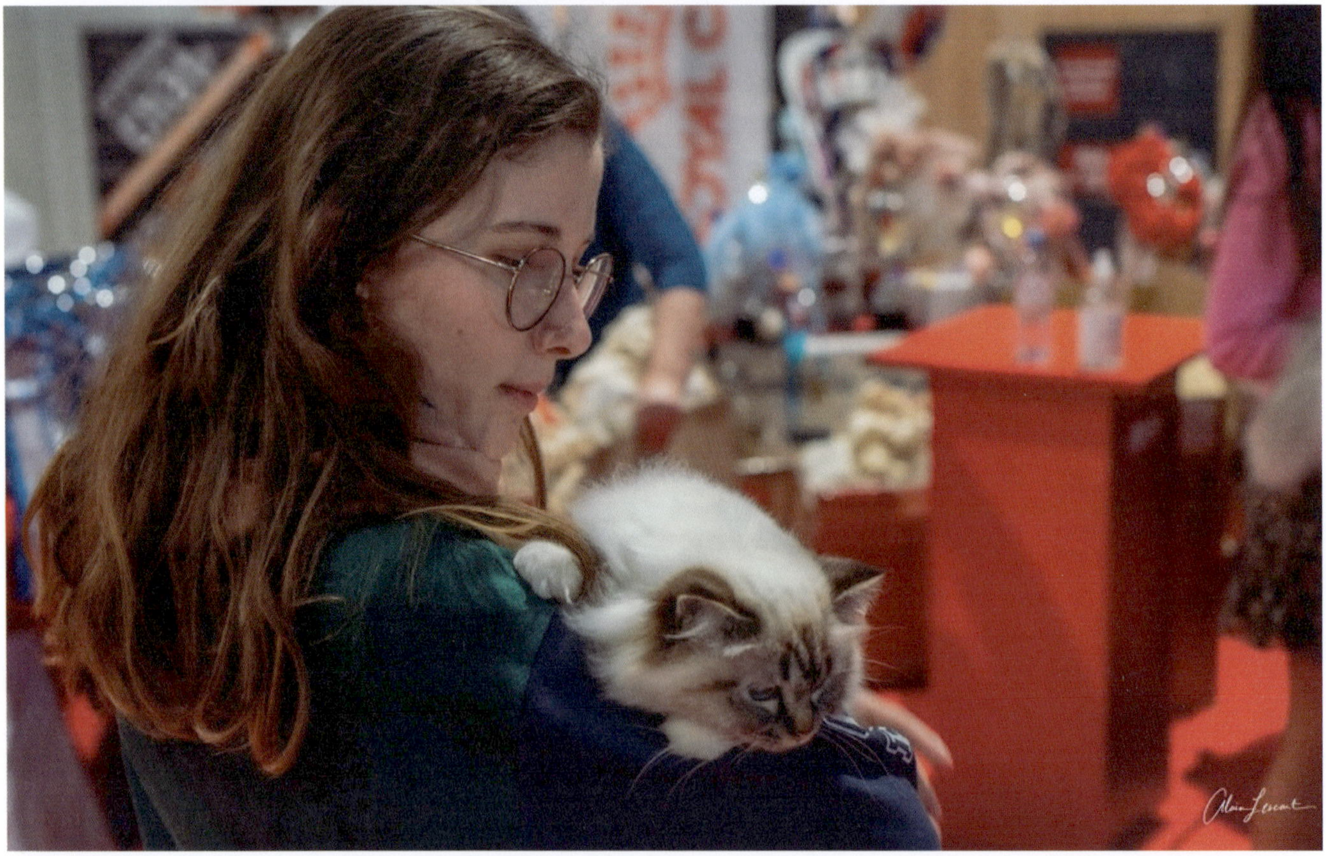

THE SACRED CAT OF BURMA CENTENNIAL

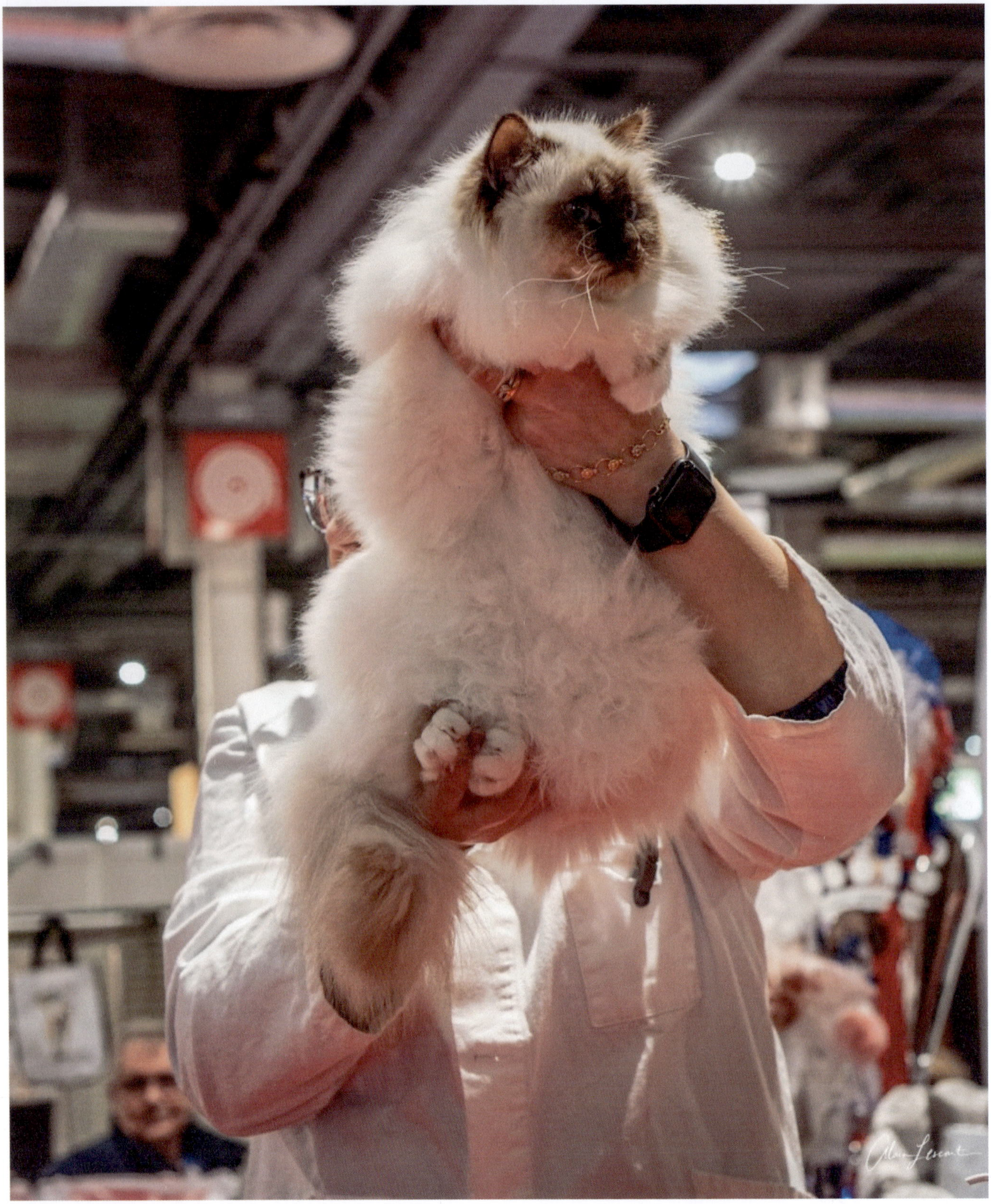

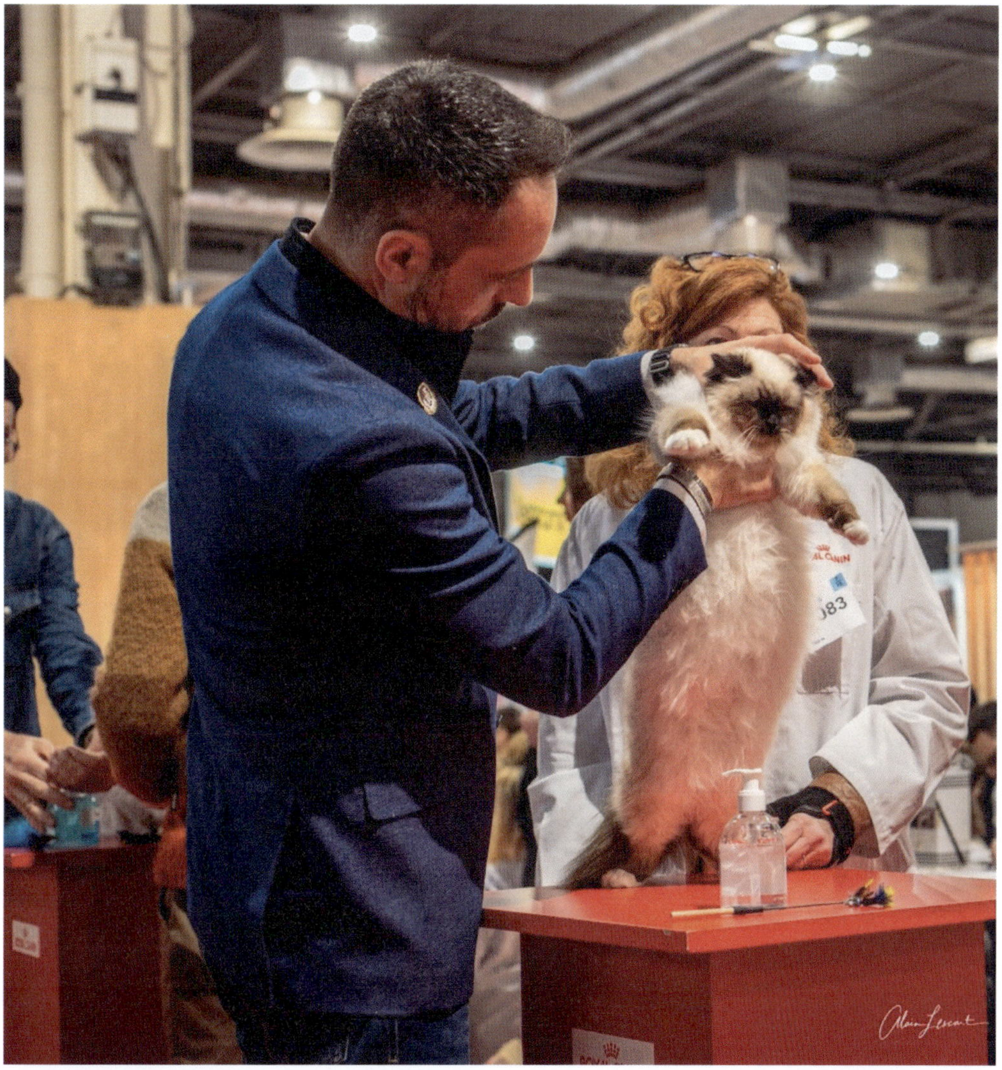

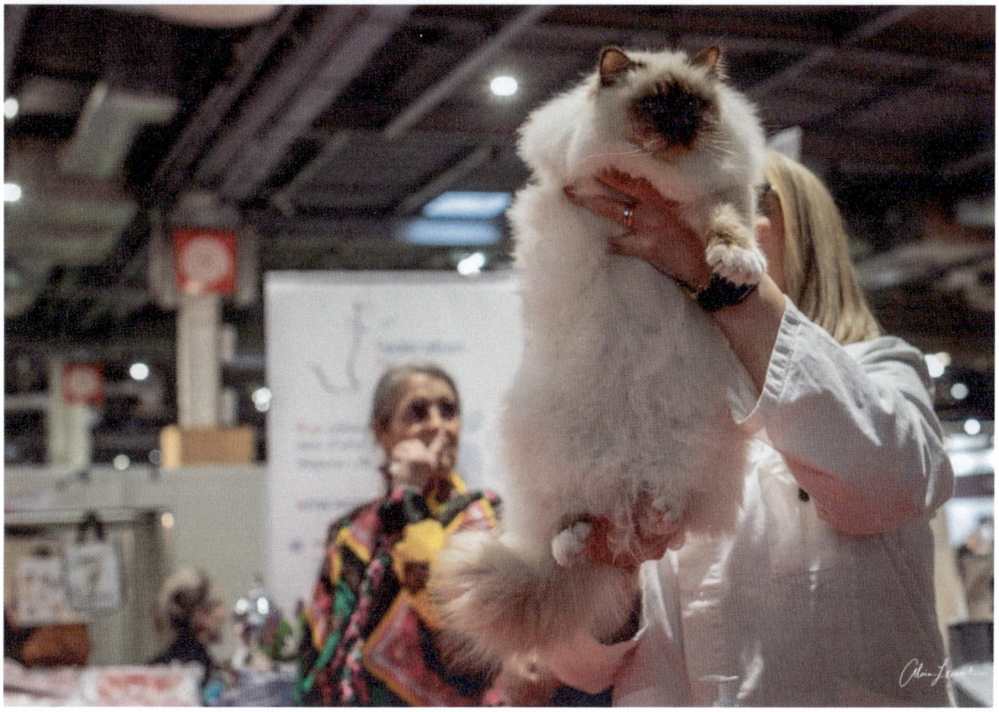

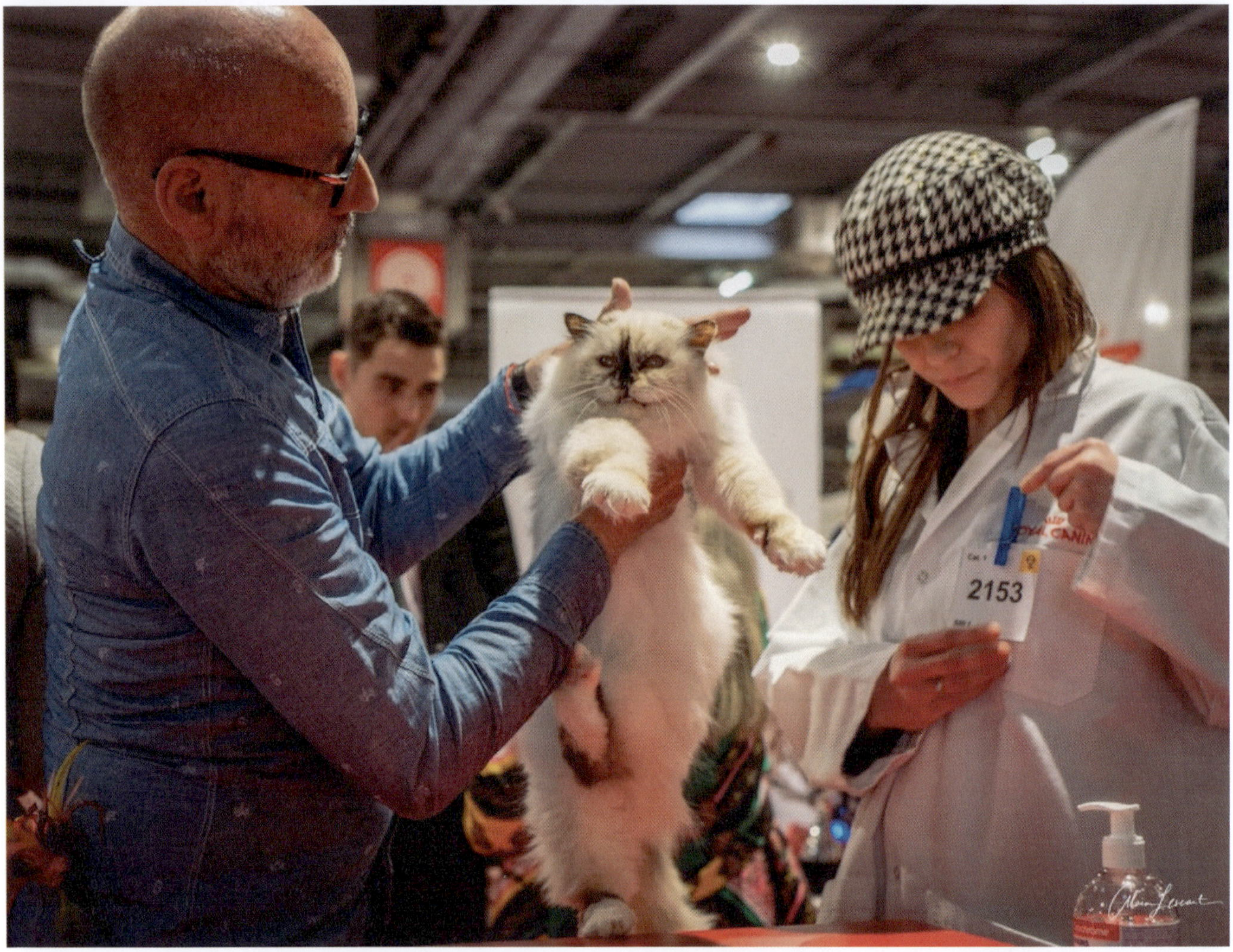
2153

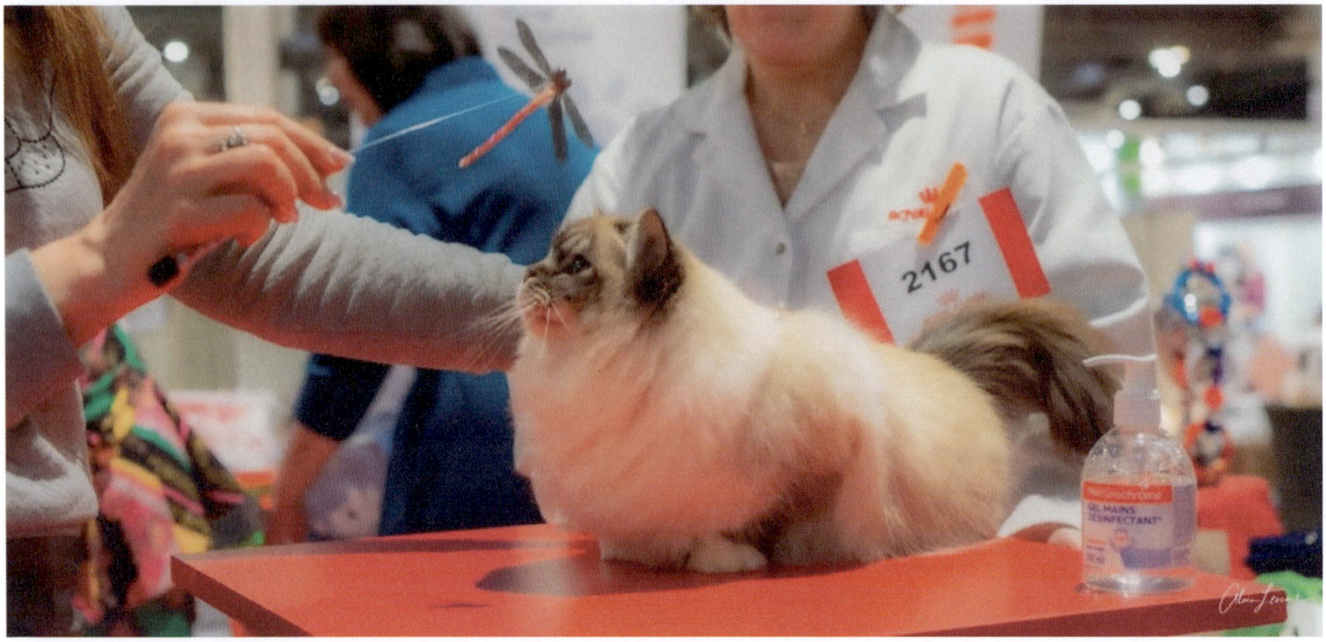
2167

THE SACRED CAT OF BURMA CENTENNIAL

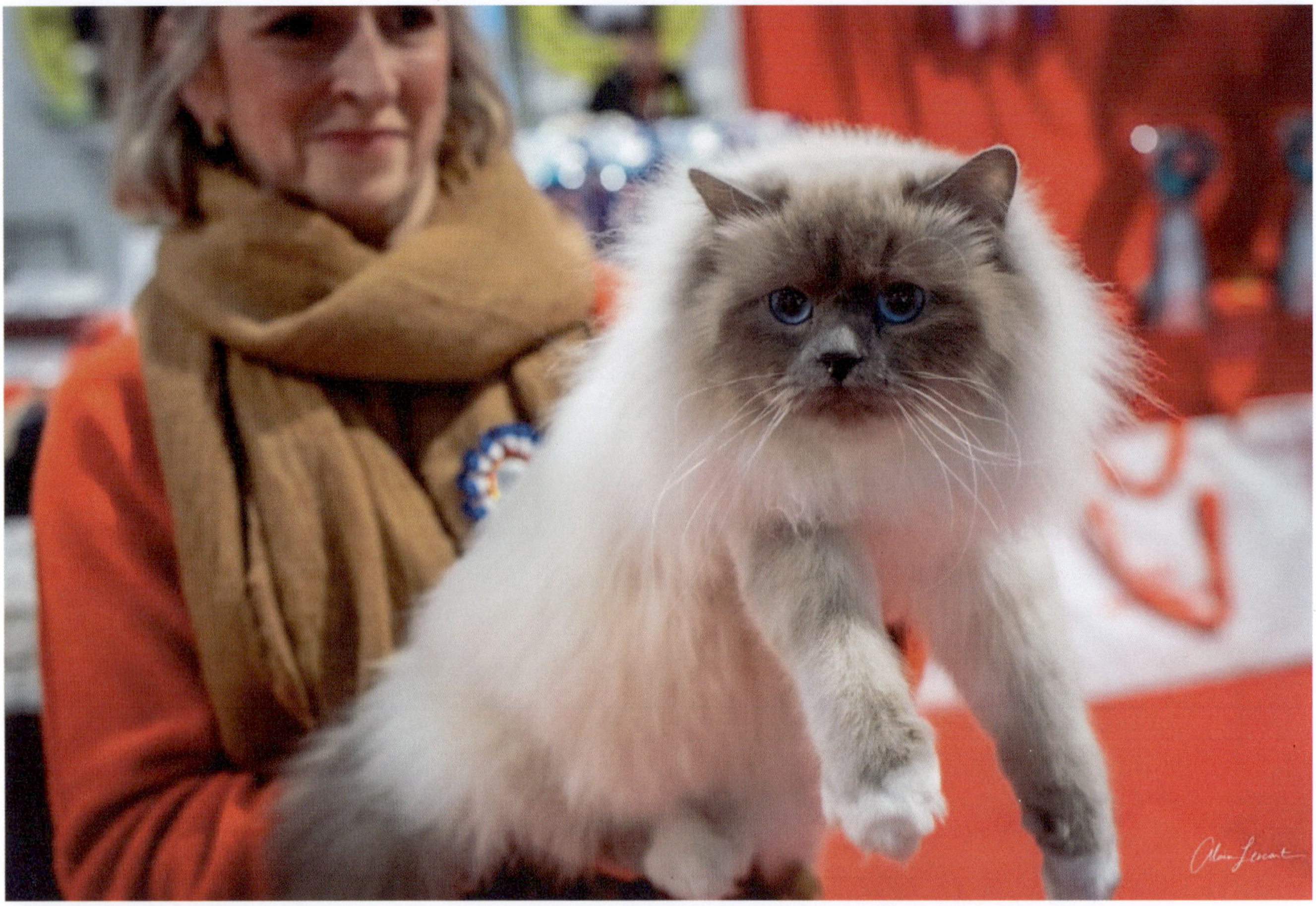

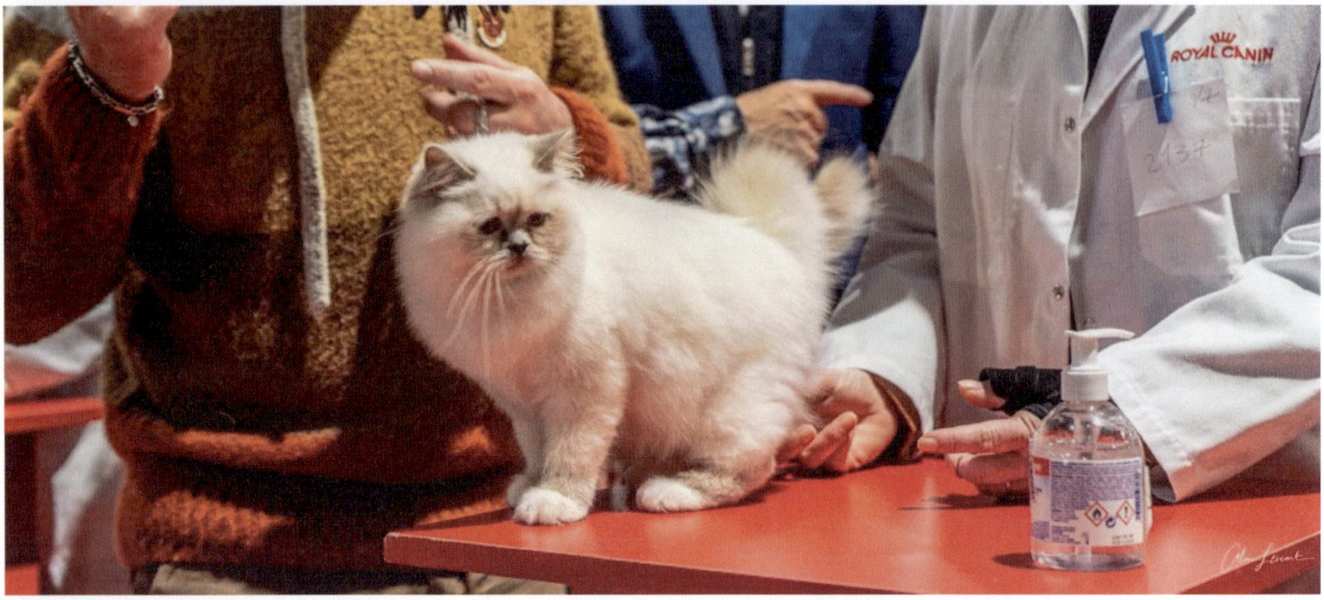
ROYAL CANIN

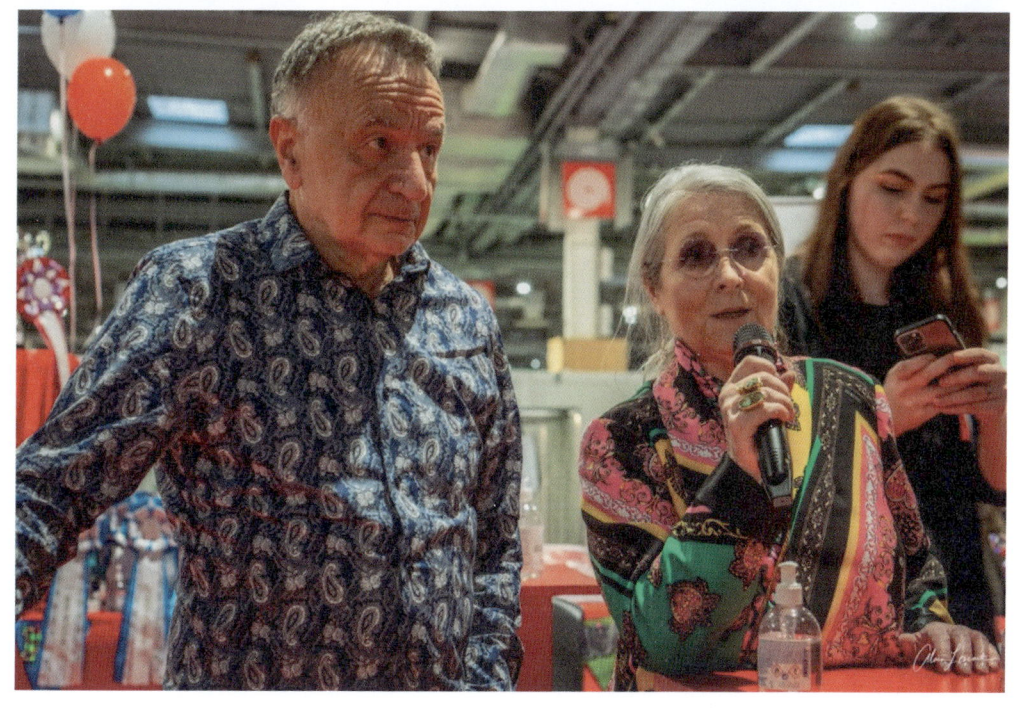

THE SACRED CAT OF BURMA CENTENNIAL

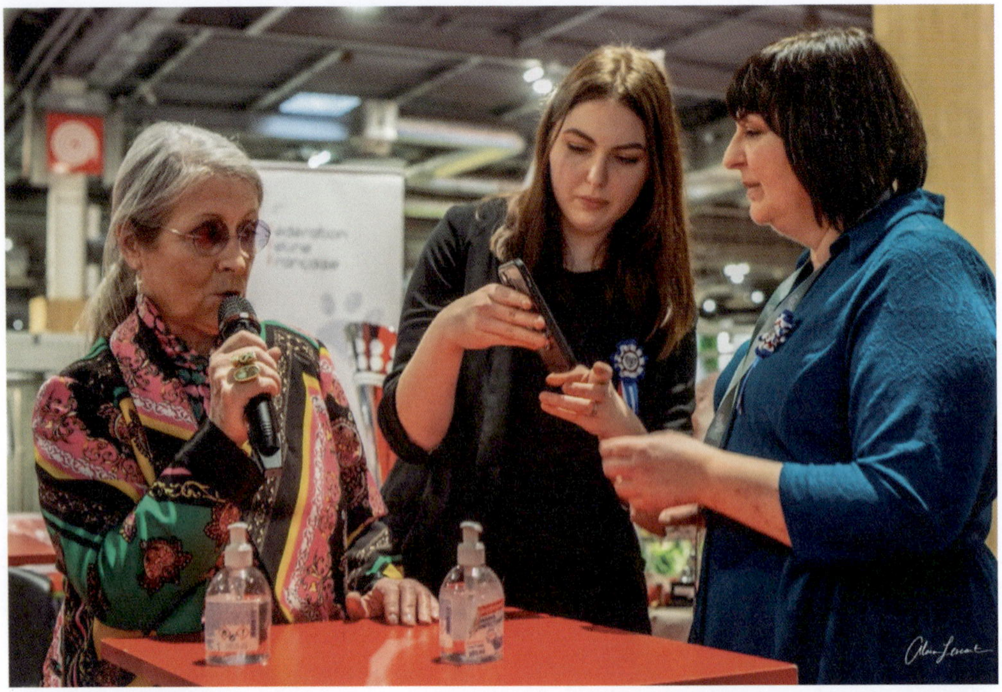

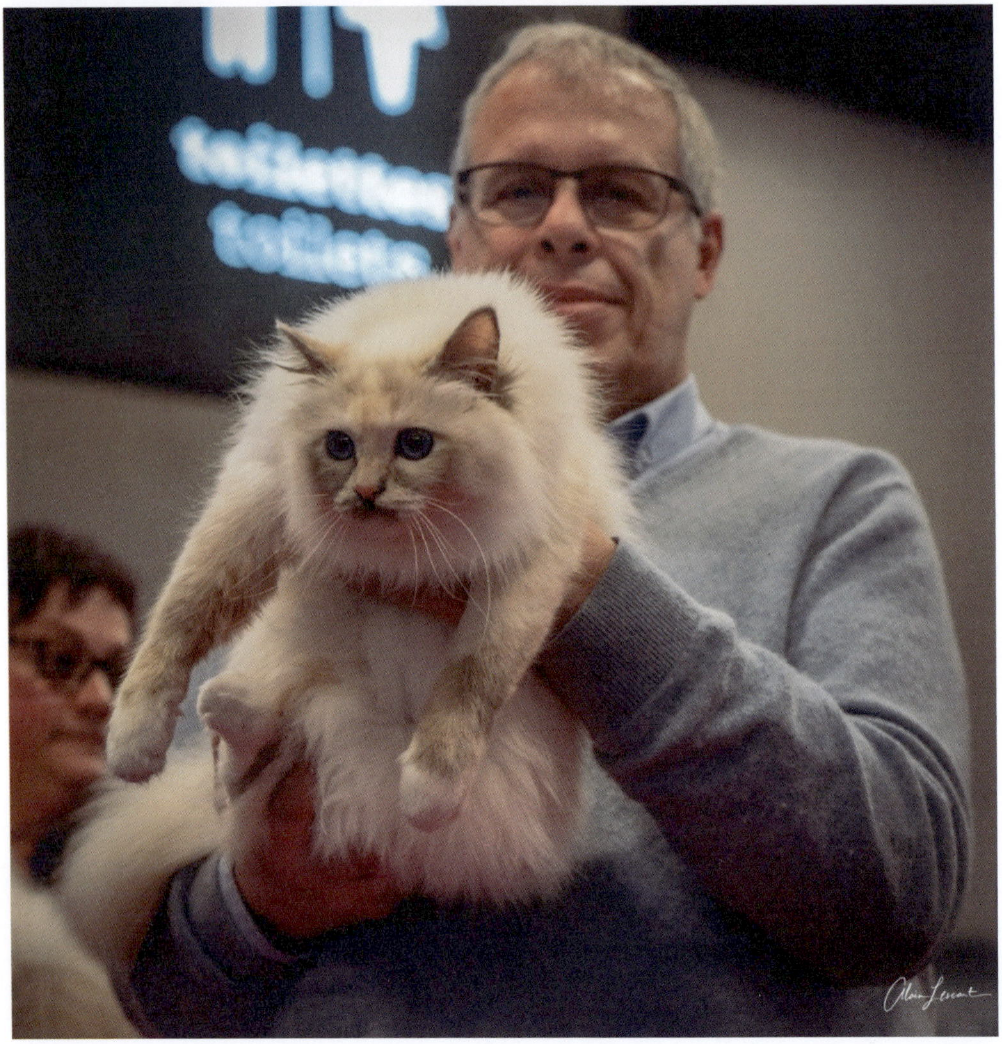

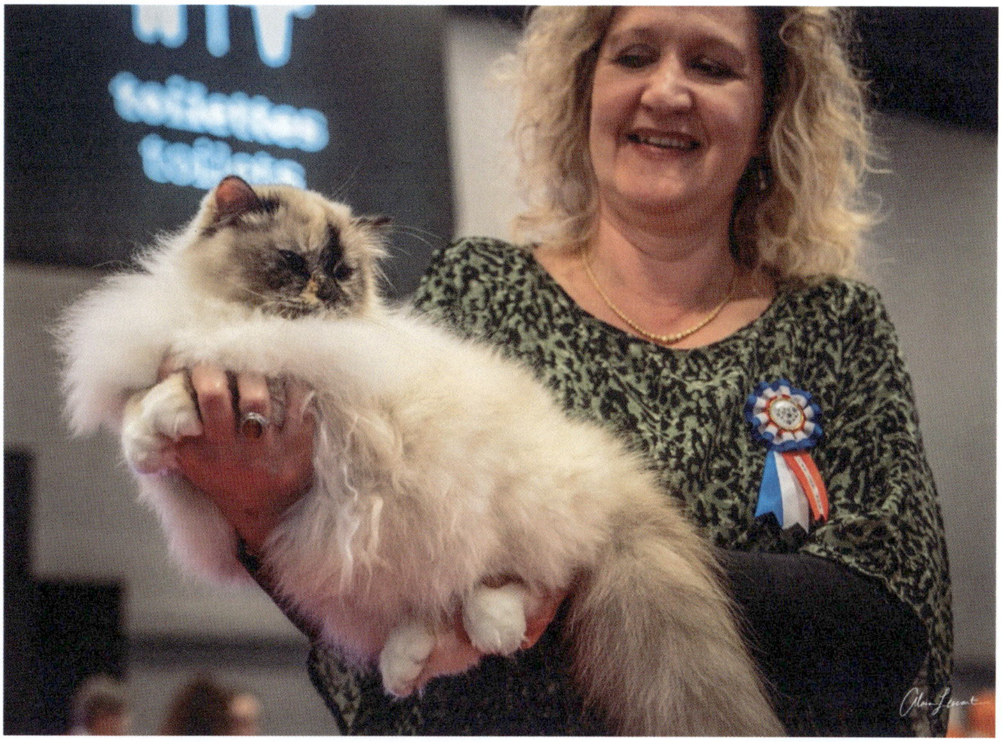
toilettes

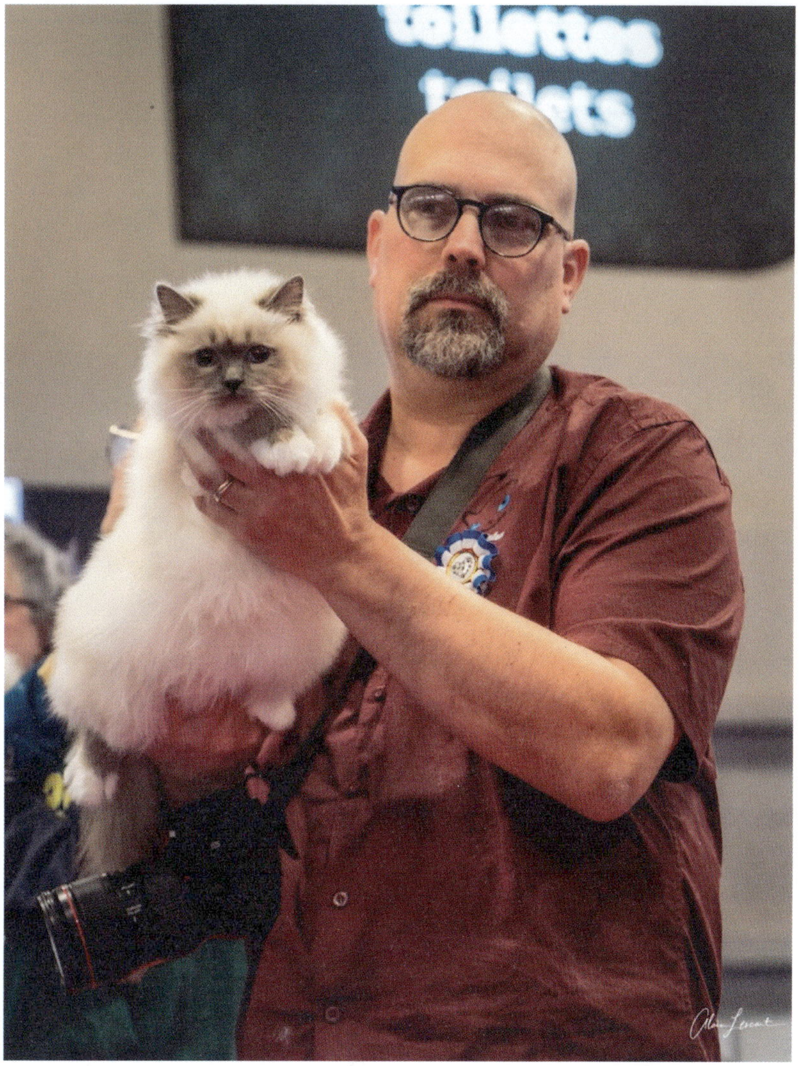

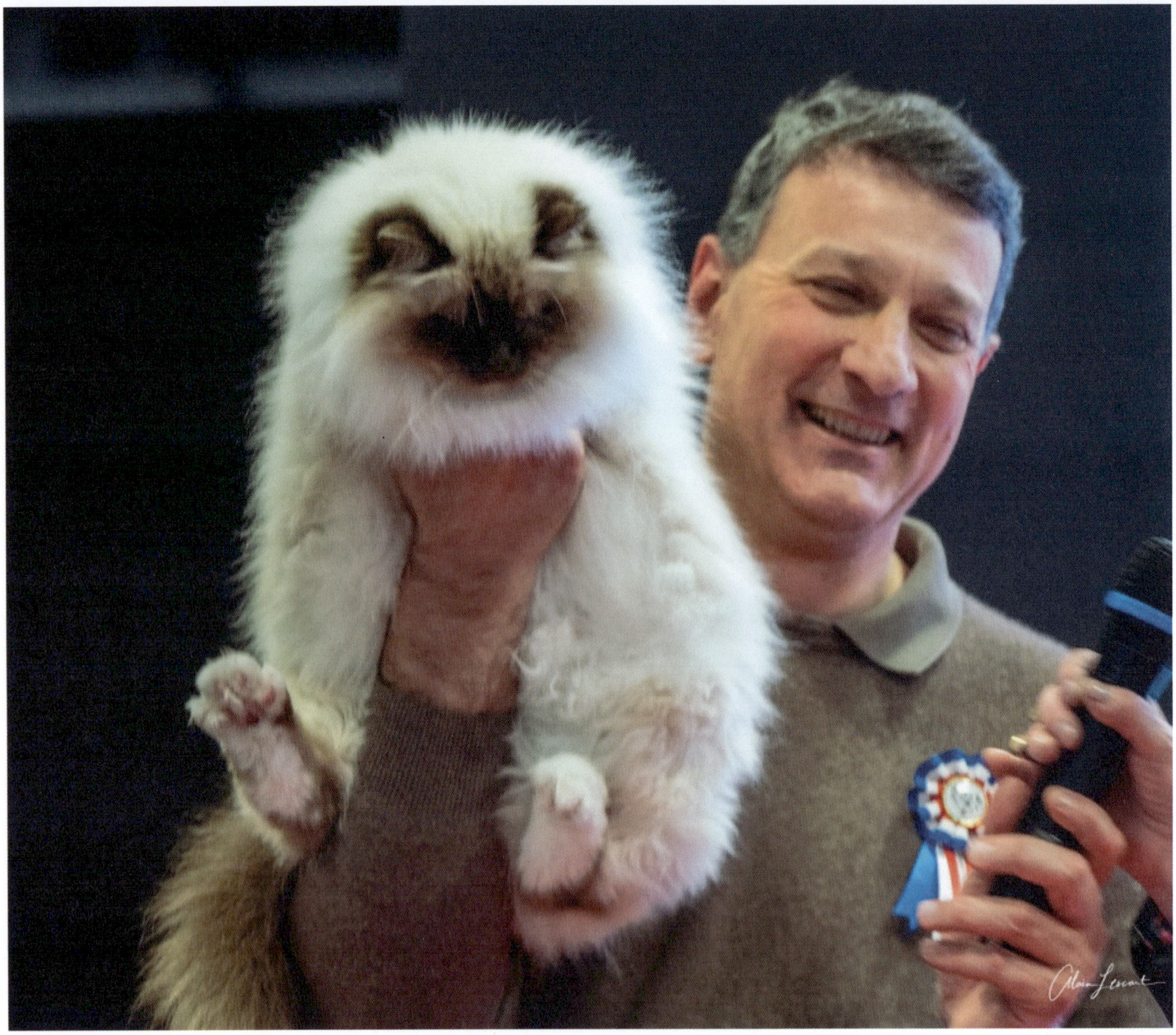

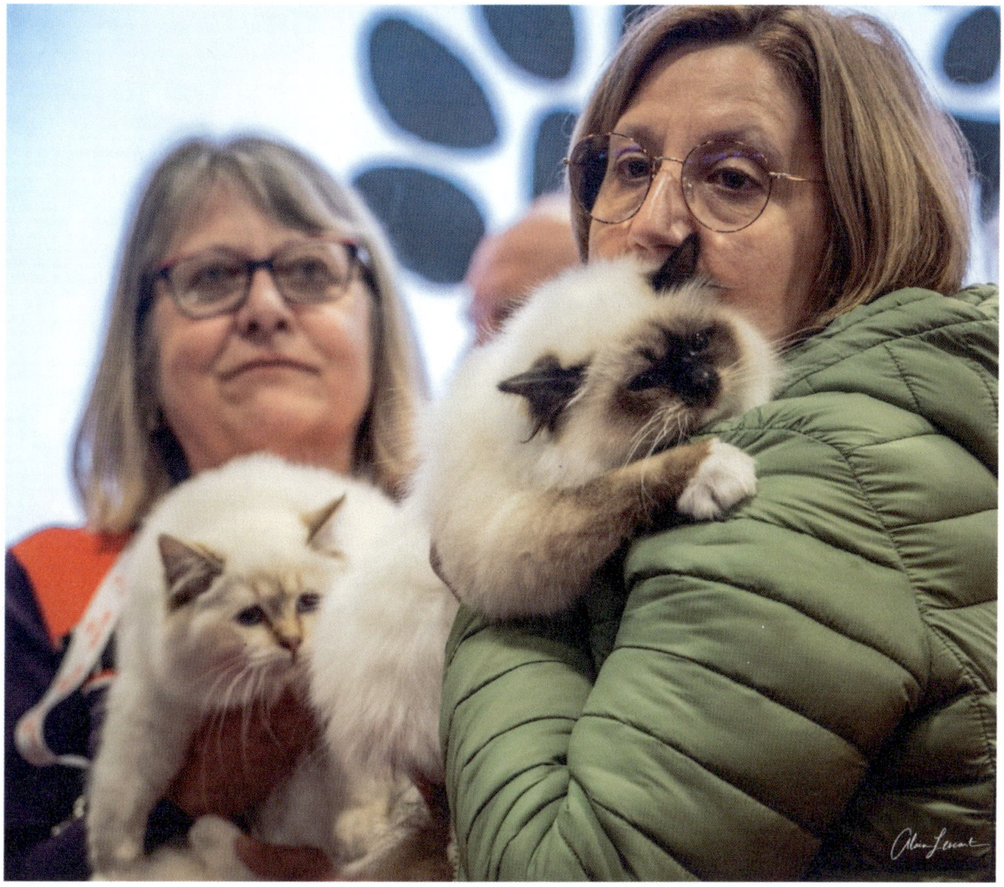

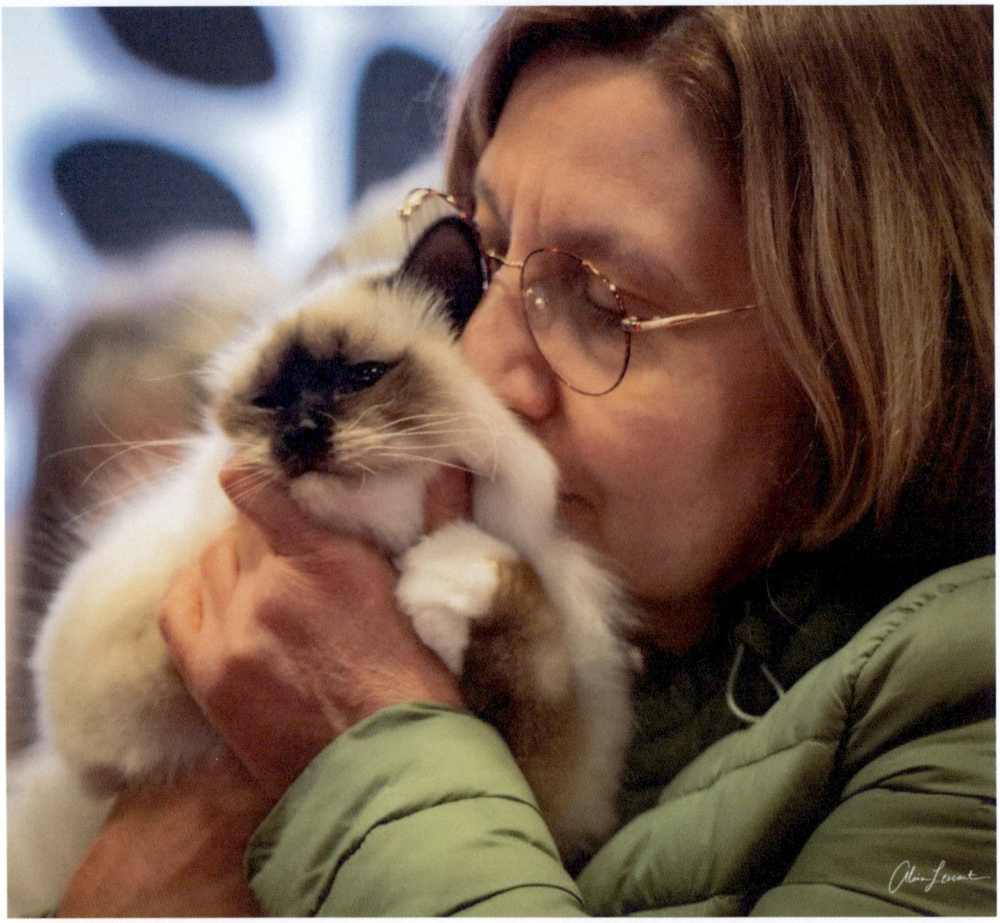

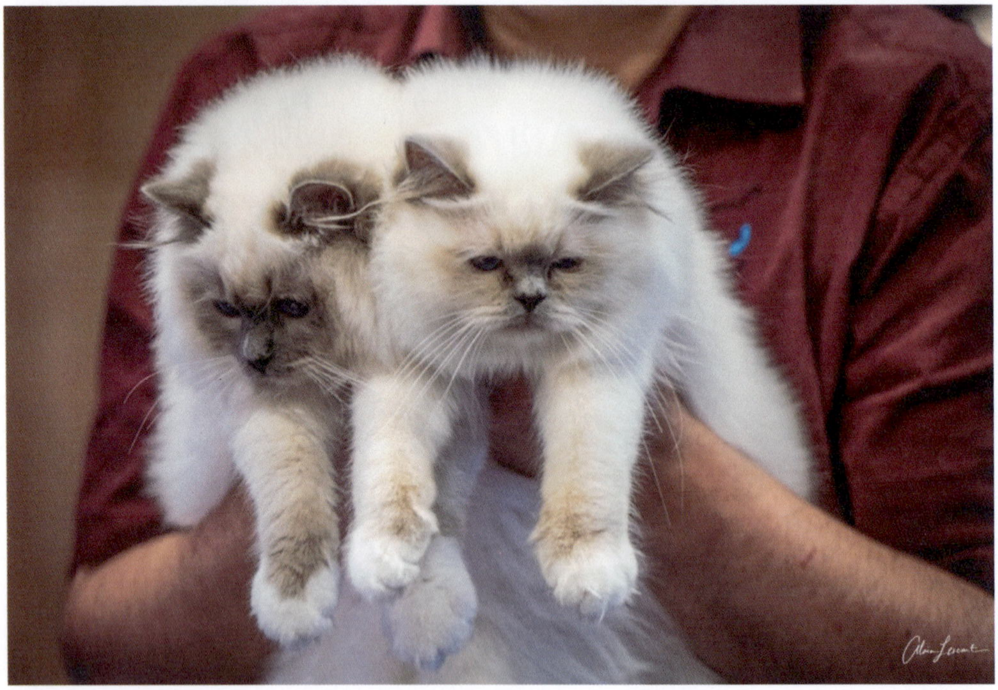

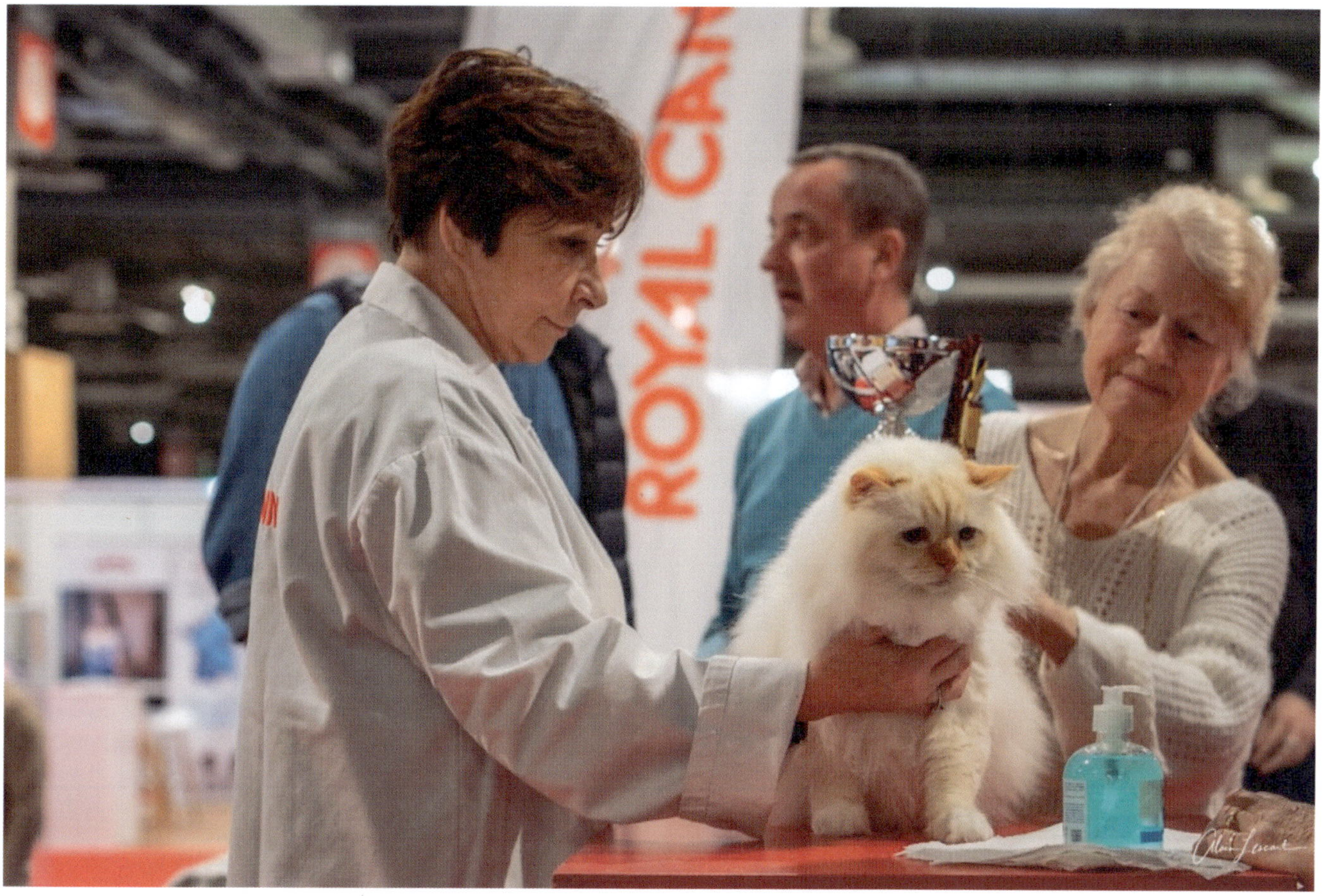
ROYAL

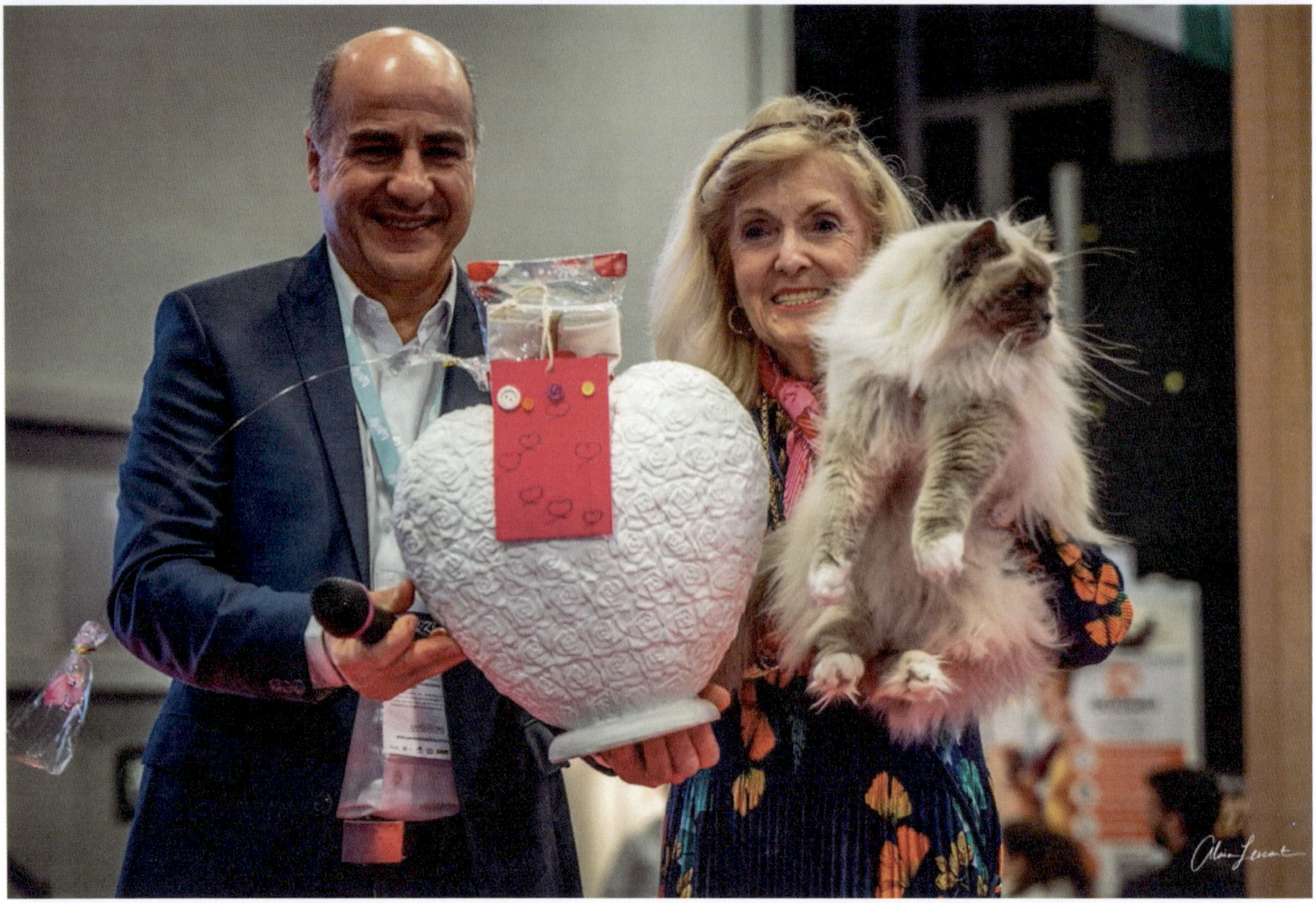
Alain Lescart

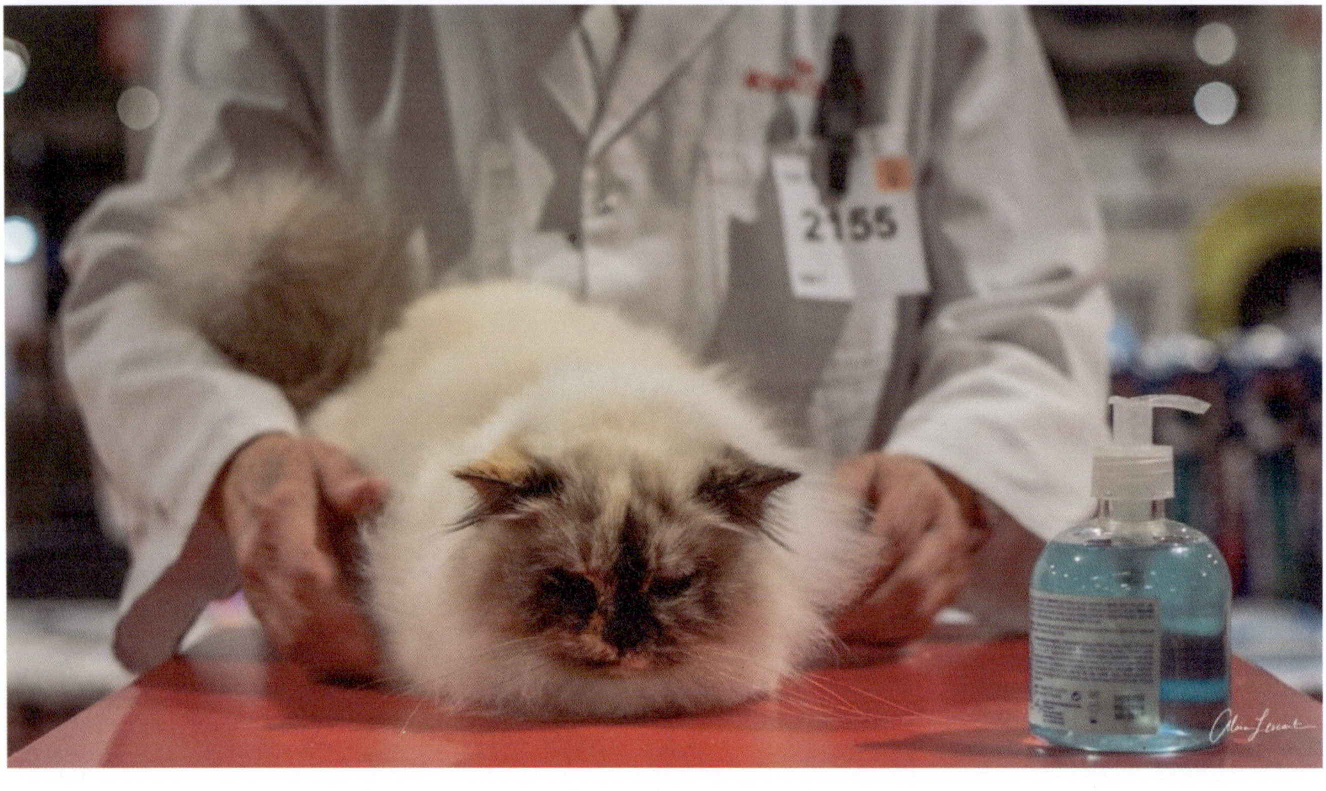
2155
Alain Lescart

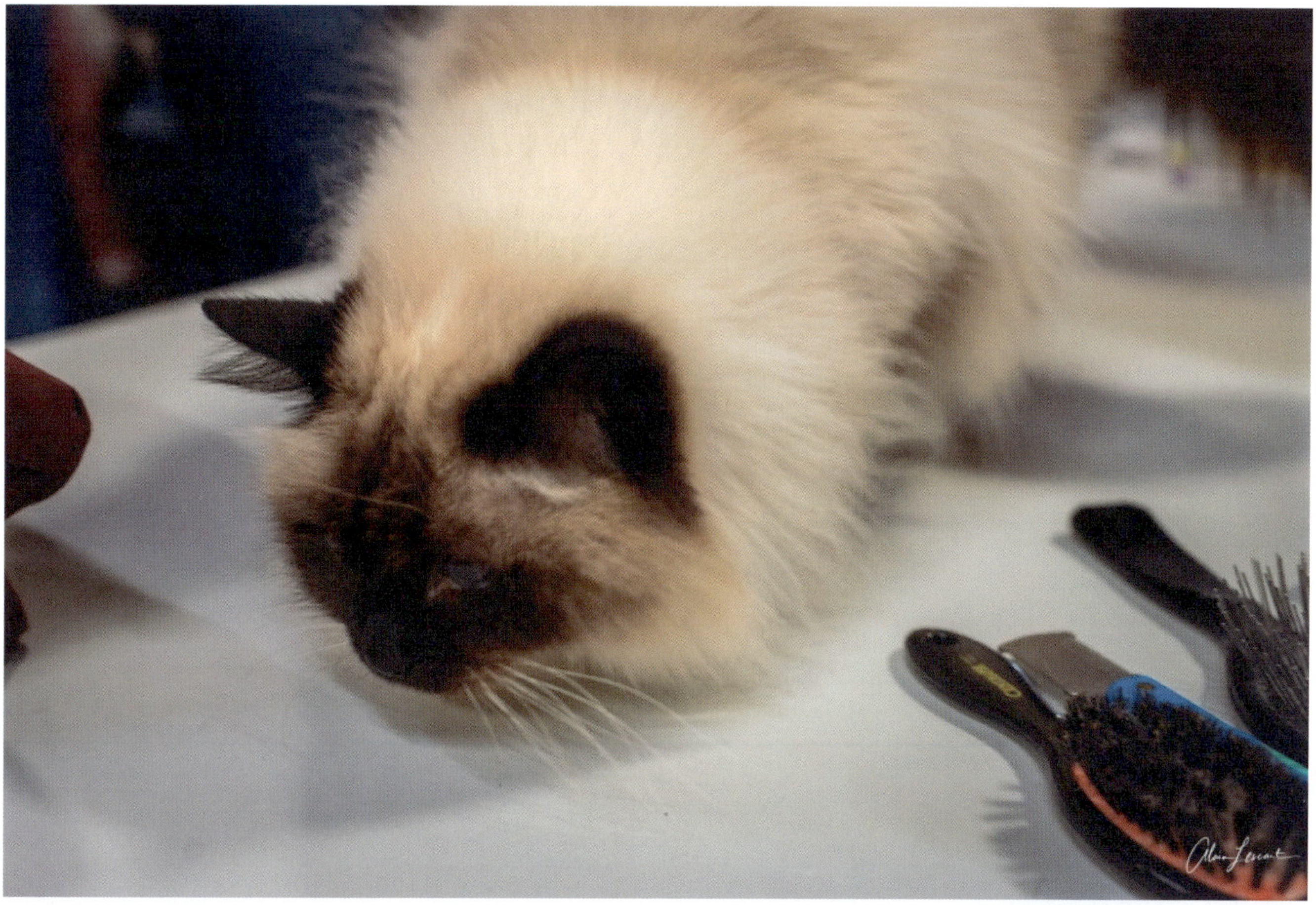

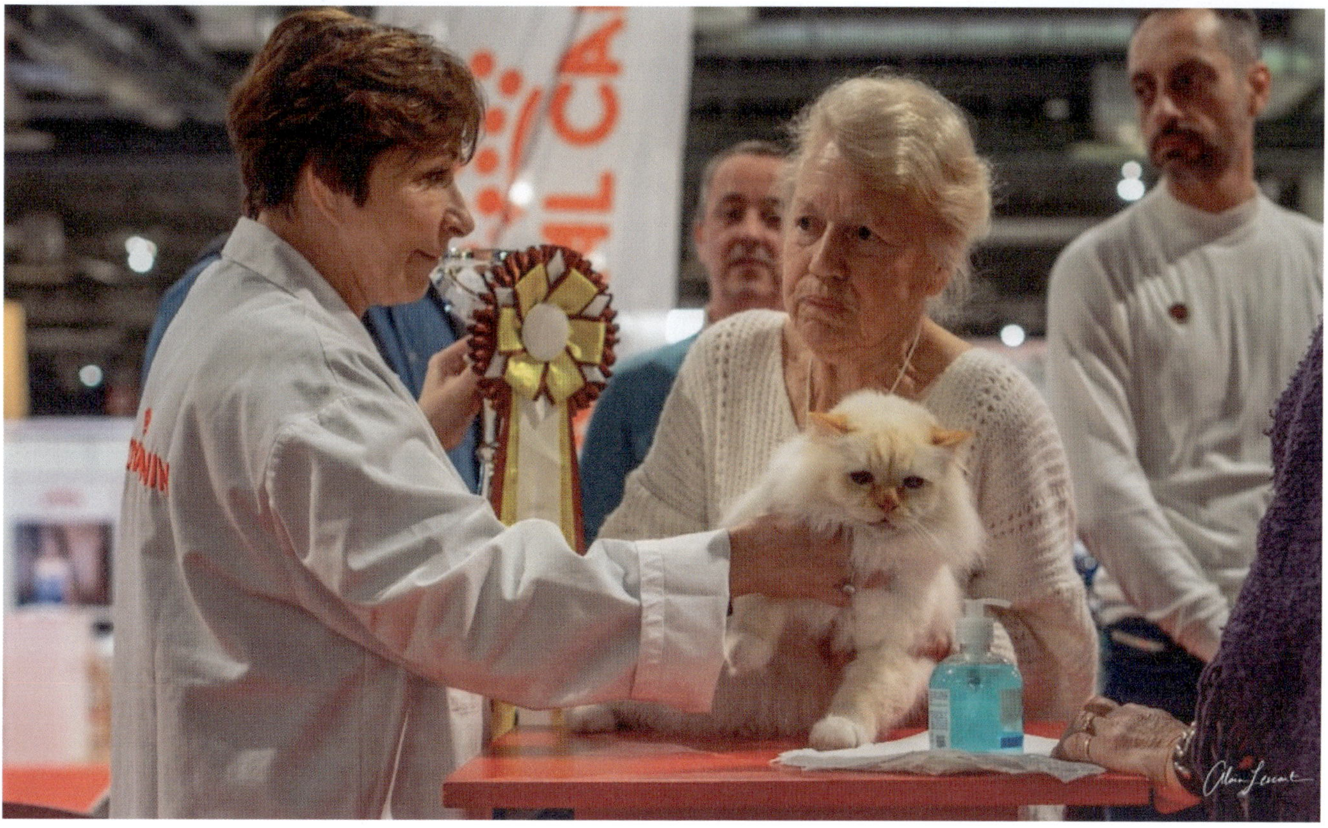

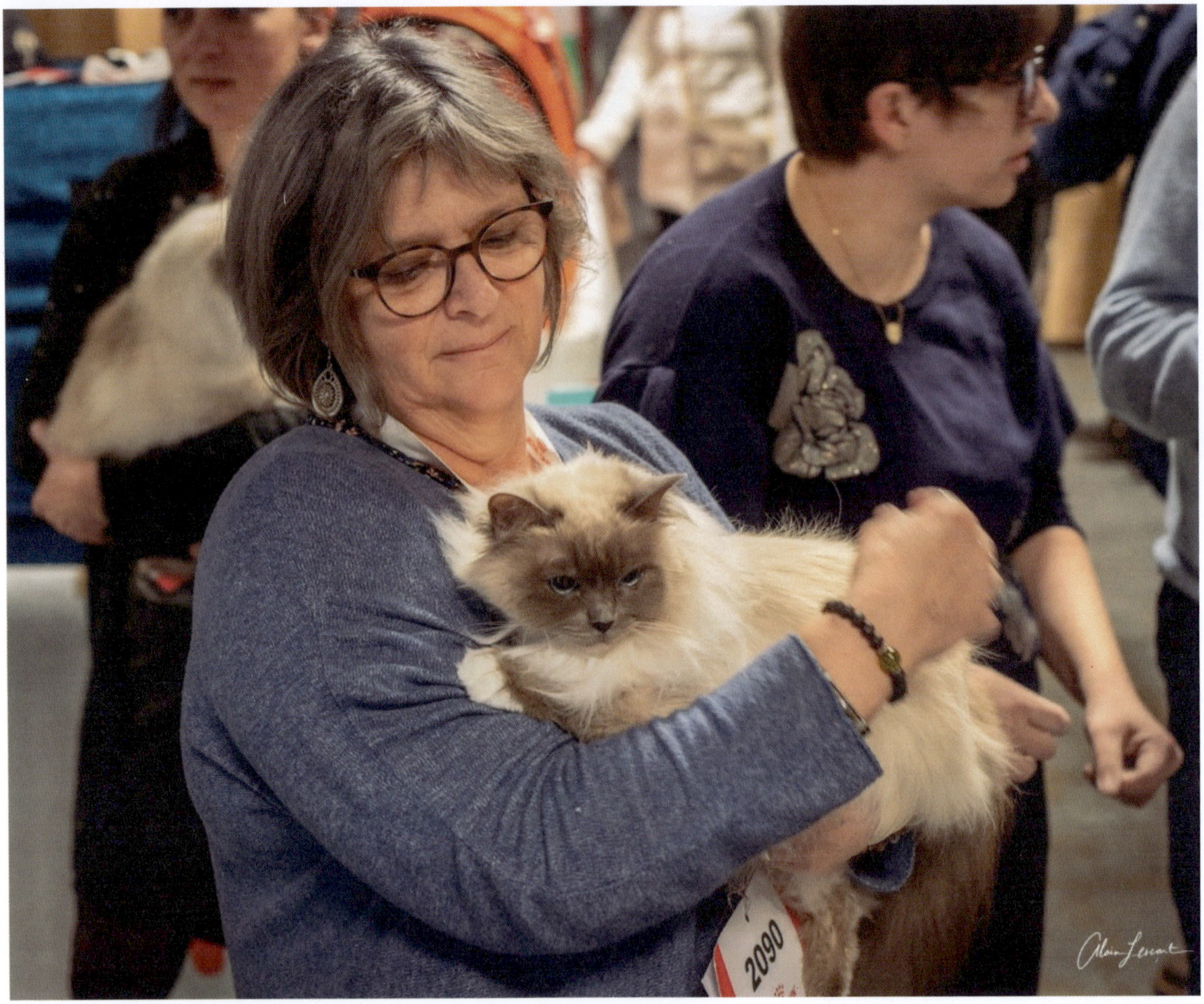
2090
Alain Lescart

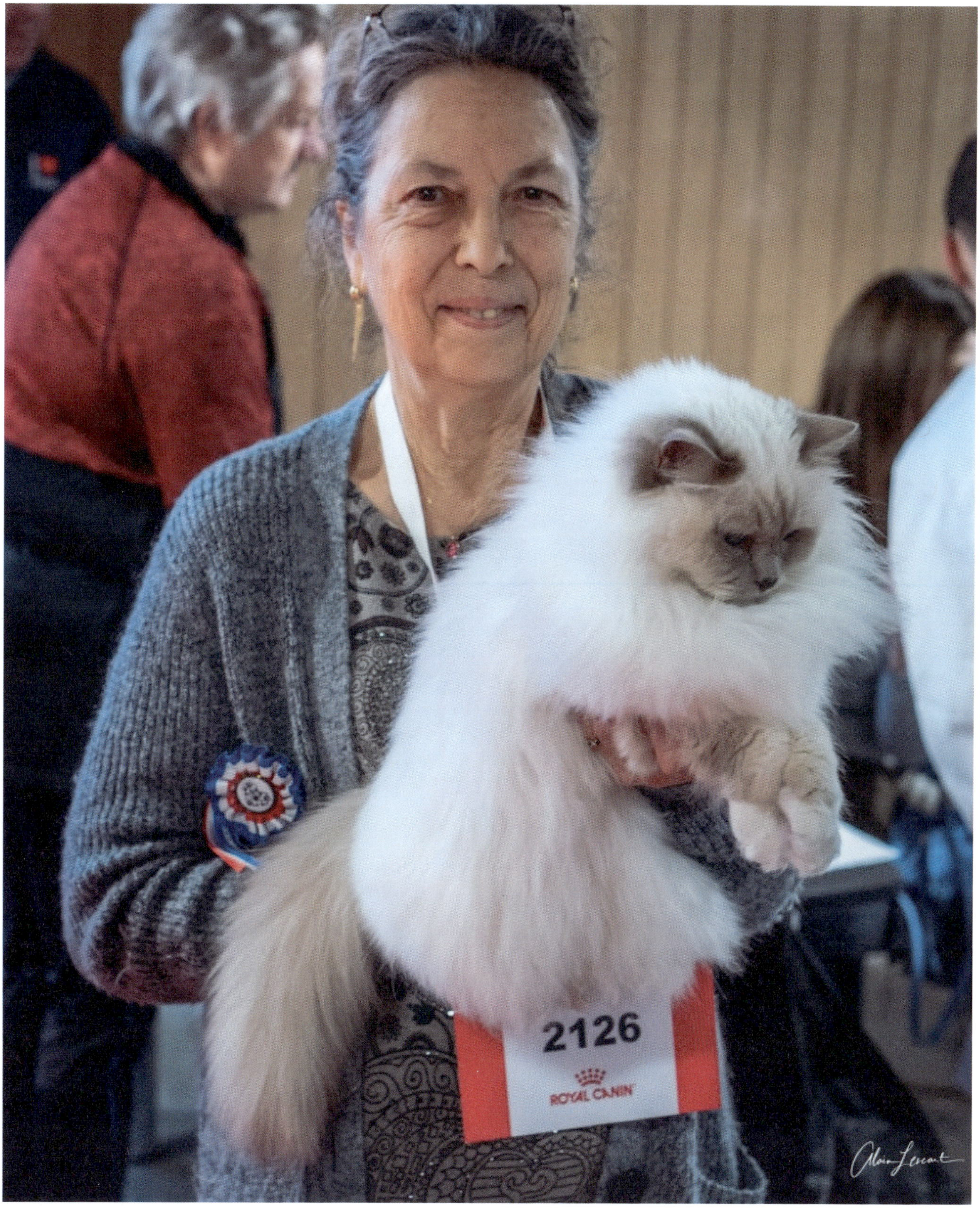
2126
ROYAL CANIN

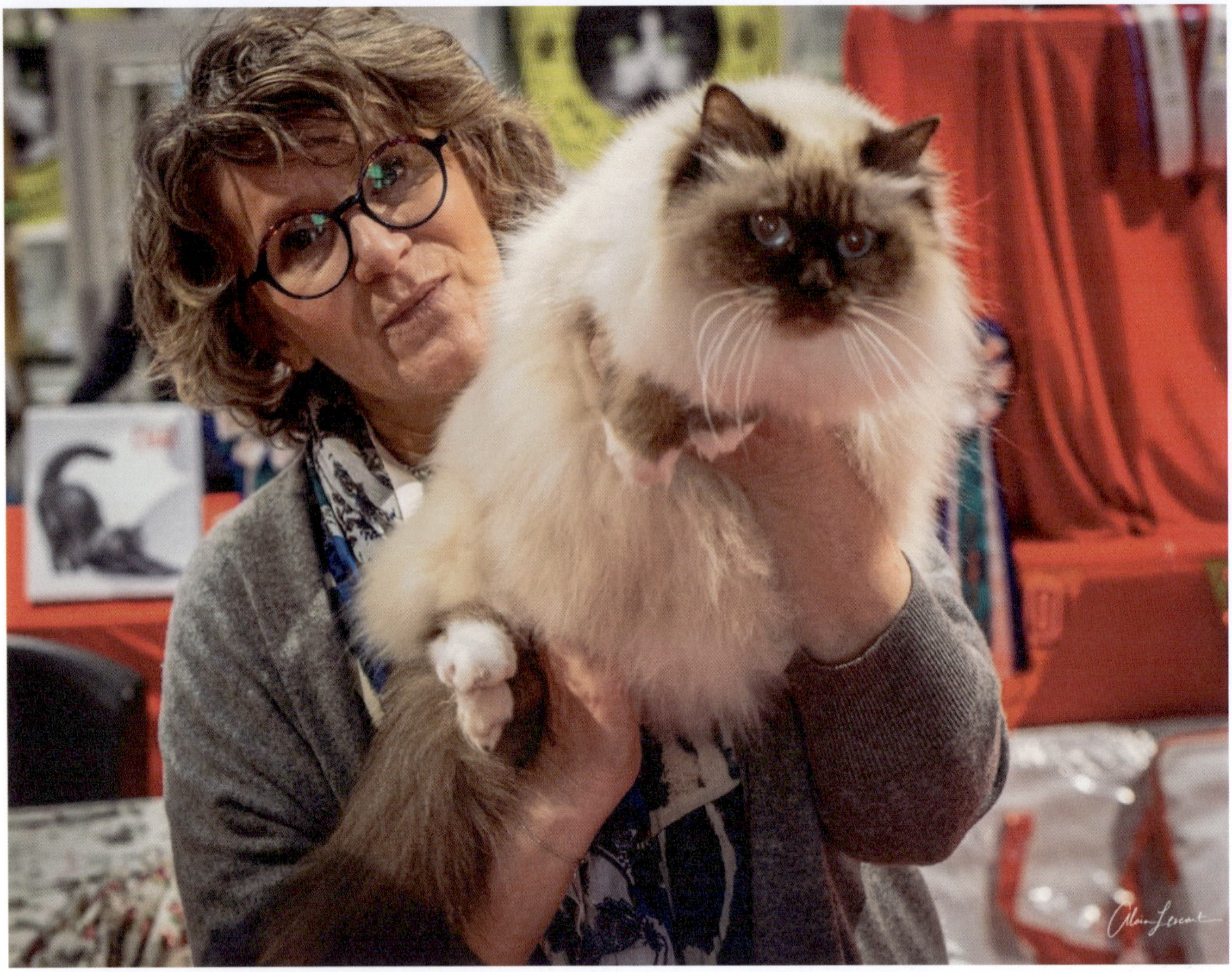

BIBLIOGRAPHY

Simpson Frances. *The Book of the Cats*. London: Cassell. 1903.

— *Cats for Pleasure and Profits*. London: Sir Isaac Pitman & Sons, LTD. 1928.

Adam Marcelle. « L'Amour qui Tremble. Roman de Marcelle Adam. Première Partie. L'amour dans les myrtes. V." Roman. » Paris: *Le Matin*, Paris: 26 décembre 1925, sec. Feuilleton 41, p. 5.

Bard Louis (rédacteur). « À quelques millions de dollars près... Le fabuleux héritage de l'Américaine. Ce que raconte Mme Léotardi, la légataire universelle. » Paris: *La Liberté*, 23 décembre 1922, 2e ed., p. 1.

Baudoin-Crevoisier Marcel. "Le Chat de Birmanie. II." *La Revue Féline Belge*. IV.2 (1931). Anvers: Les Amis du Chat. p. 6-7.

---. "Le Chat Sacré de Birmanie." *La Revue Féline Belge*. 11 & 12 (1931). Anvers: Les Amis du Chat. p. 4-6.

Jumaud Philippe. *Les races de chats*. Saint Raphaël: Ed. des Tablettes. 1925.

Alain Lescart. *L'Extraordinaire aventure du chat sacré de Birmanie*. Paris: Ed. Les Trois Colonnes. 2020.

Reney Marcel, and Marcel Abbé Chamonin. *Nos amis les chats*. Genève: Ch. Grasset, 1947.

Labgenvet. Université de Montréal. *Génétique du chat 2,0 : Les Couleurs*. https://labgenvet.ca/genetique-du-chat-2-0-les-couleurs/ December 9, 2023.

BOOKS IN THIS SERIES

The Extraordinary Adventure of the Sacred Cat of Burma

Before 1940, the sacred Cat of Birma was the most expensive cat in the world, due to its alleged rarity and its favor with the wealthy French class. From the first mention of this feline in 1922, and although the veracity of its Burmese tale was quickly questioned, no one had succeeded in uncovering the truth about its origins. Dr Alain Lescart, scholar and breeder of Birman cats, managed to uncover significant details on this subject while revealing the behind the scenes of a now forgotten legal case which made the front page of all French newspapers of the time, and which revolved around Mme Juanita Léotardi, the first breeder of Birman, and a major mythomaniac. In his work, the author follows the evolution of the legend with its inconsistencies and contradictions. He is finally interested in the difficulties encountered by the first breeders to develop the breed in the years preceding the Second World War.

L'aventure Extraordinaire Du Chat Sacré De Birmanie

BOOKS BY THIS AUTHOR

The Extraordinary Adventure Of The Sacred Cat Of Burma

Before 1940, the sacred Cat of Birma was the most expensive cat in the world, due to its alleged rarity and its favor with the wealthy French class. From the first mention of this feline in 1922, and although the veracity of its Burmese tale was quickly questioned, no one had succeeded in uncovering the truth about its origins. Dr Alain Lescart, scholar and breeder of Birman cats, managed to uncover significant details on this subject while revealing the behind the scenes of a now forgotten legal case which made the front page of all French newspapers of the time, and which revolved around Mme Juanita Léotardi, the first breeder of Birman, and a major mythomaniac. In his work, the author follows the evolution of the legend with its inconsistencies and contradictions. He is finally interested in the difficulties encountered by the first breeders to develop the breed in the years preceding the Second World War.

Cybernica

Le Professeur Tanaka rêve de créer un androïde avec un chat androïde pour compagnon, le duo parfait, dans le but ultime d'envoyer une nouvelle humanité vers une planète habitable dans l'espace. Cependant, il se heurte à de nombreuses entraves dans une société où seuls les privilégiés et les nantis sont autorisés à participer à cette mission. Dans cette aventure captivante, suivez le Professeur Iiashi dans sa quête pour briser les barrières de la société et offrir une chance à tous de repartir à zéro sur une nouvelle planète. "Le Voyage Interstellaire de l'Androïde et du Chat" est une histoire de détermination, de persévérance et de l'espoir de réinventer l'humanité. Une exploration audacieuse de l'égalité et de l'inclusion dans un avenir lointain.

ABOUT THE AUTHOR

Alain Lescart

Dr. Alain Lescart is a university professor in California where he teaches French and Literature. His specialty is XIXth century French Literature and XXTh Century culture. He also specialized in Fantasy Literature.

As a Birman breeder since 1986, he has spent part of his research studying the origin of the Birman cat.

Printed in Poland
by Amazon Fulfillment
Poland Sp. z o.o., Wrocław
27 December 2023